THE WAY, THE TRUTH AND THE LIFE

Theological Resources for a Pilgrimage to a Global Anglican Future

PREPARED BY THE
THEOLOGICAL RESOURCE TEAM OF
GAFCON

The Latimer Trust

REGENT COLLEGE PUBLISHING
Vancouver, British Columbia

This edition published 2008 by special arrangement with the

Latimer Trust
PO Box 26685
London N14 4XQ
www.latimertrust.org

Regent College Publishing
5800 University Boulevard
Vancouver, British Columbia
V6T 2E4 Canada
Web: www.regentpublishing.com
E-mail: info@regentpublishing.com

Cover photograph: "Jerusalem alley" © mr.lightning – Fotolia.com

Library and Archives Canada Cataloguing in Publication

   The way, the truth and the life : theological resources for a pilgrimage to a global Anglican future / prepared by the Theological Resource Team of the Global Anglican Future Conference (GAFCON) ; editors, Vinay Samuel, Chris Sugden and Sarah Finch.

Co-published by: Latimer Trust.
Includes bibliographical references.
ISBN 978-1-57383-429-2

   1. Anglican Communion. 2. Anglican Communion—Doctrines.
I. Samuel, Vinay II. Sugden, Chris III. Finch, Sarah IV. Latimer Trust
V. Global Anglican Future Conference (2008 : Jerusalem, Israel)

BX5005.W39 2008   230'.3   C2008-906047-4

THE THEOLOGICAL RESOURCE GROUP OF THE GLOBAL ANGLICAN FUTURE CONFERENCE AND PILGRIMAGE

Chairman: Archbishop Nicholas Okoh, *Bishop of Asaba and Archbishop of Bendel, Nigeria*

Convenor: Canon Dr Vinay Samuel, *South India*

Archbishop Bennett Okoro, *Bishop of Orlu and Archbishop of Owerri, Nigeria*

Bishop Onuoha, *Bishop of Okigwe, South Nigeria*

Bishop Simeon Adebola, *Bishop of Yewa, Nigeria*

Bishop John Akao, *Bishop of Sabongidda-Ora, Nigeria*

Professor Dapo Asaju, *Department of Religious Studies, Lagos State University, Nigeria*

Canon Festus Yeboah-Asuamah, *Kwame Nkrumah University of Science and Technology, Ghana*

Revd Roger Beckwith, *England*

Bishop Wallace Benn, *Bishop of Lewes, England*

Bishop Robinson Cavalcanti, *Bishop of Recife, Brazil, Southern Cone*

Bishop John Ellison, *former Bishop of Paraguay*

Bishop Michael Fape, *Bishop of Remo, Nigeria*

Dr Steven Ferguson, *USA*

Canon Alistair Macdonald-Radcliff, *sometime Dean of All Saints Cathedral, Cairo, Egypt*

Revd Professor Stephen Noll, *Vice Chancellor, Uganda Christian University*

Bishop Ikechi Nwosu, *Bishop of Umuahia, Nigeria*

Bishop Joel Obetia, *Bishop of Madi and West Nile, Uganda*

Revd Dr Emily Onyango, *St Paul's University, Limuru. Kenya*

Revd Dr Mike Ovey, *Principal of Oak Hill Theological College, England*

Revd Dr Mark Thompson, *Head of Theology and Academic Dean, Moore Theological College, Sydney, Australia*

Bishop Eliud Wabukala, *Chair of National Council of Churches, Bishop of Bungoma, Kenya*

Editor: Mrs Sarah Finch, *Member of General Synod, England*

Secretary: Canon Dr Chris Sugden, *England*

Contents

Four Current Concerns

Preface

The Most Revd Nicholas D. Okoh
Archbishop of Bendel, Nigeria
Chairman, GAFCON Theological Resource Team

The decision to write this handbook, to serve as a theological introduction and definition for GAFCON, was reached on the same day, 14 December 2007, in Nairobi, that the leadership team resolved to organize GAFCON. The opening section, *A most agonizing journey towards Lambeth 2008*, explains how, in recent years, huge amounts of time, energy and money have been expended, in the search for an agreeable solution to the human sexuality controversy in the Anglican Communion. It has remained elusive.

In the course of time, it became clear that the issue at stake was much wider than the human sexuality issue concerning same-sex unions. What had been 'in the works' for some years – the challenge to the authority of the Bible, in all matters of faith and practice, both within the Church and in personal morality – suddenly became a public reality when, in 2003, Gene Robinson, a practising homosexual, was consecrated bishop in the United States of America. Later, in 2006, The Council of Anglican Provinces in Africa (CAPA) produced a positional paper, *The Road to Lambeth*, which identified a crisis of doctrine and also of leadership, observing correctly that the Anglican Communion was at a crossroads; it had to decide, without further hesitation, which way to go. One road, that of compromising Biblical truth, would lead to destruction and disunity. The other road might have its own obstacles, but it would lead to God and to life. It is this second road that has brought us to GAFCON.

What beliefs do GAFCON Anglicans hold? These papers, written by members of the GAFCON Theological Resource Team, reaffirm our Christian faith as it relates to some prime topics: Anglican identity and orthodoxy, the Lordship of Jesus Christ and its implications for personal morality and in mission, and the whole issue of authority, Christ's authority in the Church and the authority of the Bible. One paper discusses the all-important issue of worship, yesterday, today and tomorrow. These and a few other subjects are briefly addressed in this collection of papers, which is a GAFCON theological handbook.

It must be admitted that the result is imperfect, for several reasons, chief of which is the time constraint. Unfortunately it was not possible to cover further aspects of theology in the time available. The book is being released in advance of GAFCON 2008, Jordan and Jerusalem, as part of our preparation for the conference. Later on it is hoped that a post-GAFCON revision, incorporating fuller discussion and more topics, will be compiled.

It is not the intention of these papers to initiate a fresh debate. We should remember how the Church in North Africa and Asia Minor almost totally disappeared, at a time when Christological debate was raging in the Church. Instead, the book is offered with the purpose of guiding and educating everyone who comes to GAFCON: bishops and their wives, clergy, and concerned lay people, including young people. So, we hope it will be found to be jargon-free and readable.

The Revd Canon Dr. Chris Sugden, our Secretary, has worked very hard from the outset. We owe a huge debt of gratitude to him, and also to our Convener, Dr. Vinay Samuel. As members of the Theological Resource Team, we have enjoyed a wonderful bond of brotherhood in the Lord, during the preparation of this handbook. And we have developed confidence in one another, which I think holds great promise for the future. As a team, we reflect the catholicity of GAFCON, having come from Kenya, Uganda, Nigeria, UK, USA, Australia and India. Here I would like to express, on behalf of the leadership team, our gratitude to our publishers, The Latimer Trust, for their readiness to work with us. Finally, all of us in the Theological Resource Team are immensely grateful to the leadership team of GAFCON for the privilege of this assignment.

A Most Agonizing Journey towards Lambeth 2008

The Most Revd Peter Akinola
Archbishop of Abuja and Primate of all Nigeria

I therefore, a prisoner for the Lord, beg you to lead a life worthy of the calling to which you have been called, with all humility and gentleness, with patience, bearing with one another in love, making every effort to maintain the unity of the Spirit in the bond of peace. (Eph. 4:1-3)

We have been on this journey for ten long years. It has been costly and debilitating for all concerned, as demonstrated most recently by the tepid response to the invitations to the proposed Lambeth Conference 2008. At a time when we should be able to gather together and celebrate remarkable stories of growth, and the many wonderful ways in which our God has been at work in our beloved Communion, with lives being transformed, new churches being built and new dioceses established, there is little enthusiasm even to meet.

There are continual cries for patience, listening and understanding. And yet the record shows that those who hold to the 'faith once and for all delivered to the saints' have shown remarkable forbearance, while their pleas have been ignored, their leaders have been demonized, and their advocates marginalized. At the Lambeth Conference in 1998 we made a deliberate, prayerful decision with regard to matters of Human Sexuality. This decision was supported by an overwhelming majority of the bishops of the Communion. It reflected traditional teaching, interpreted with pastoral sensitivity. And yet it has been ignored, and those who uphold it have been derided for their stubbornness. However, we have continued to meet and pray and struggle to find ways to maintain the unity of the Spirit in the bond of peace.

The journey started in February 1997 in Kuala Lumpur. It was here, during the 2nd Encounter of the Global South Anglican Communion, that a statement was issued expressing concern about the apparent setting aside of Biblical teaching by some provinces and dioceses. The statement pleaded for dialogue in 'a spirit of true unity' before any part of the Communion embarked on radical changes to Church discipline and moral teaching.

Sadly, this plea, as with several similar warnings, has been ignored. Ten years later, in February 2007, the Primates of the Anglican Communion met in Dar es Salaam, Tanzania, and experienced an agonizing time as they tried to repair the Communion that had been so badly broken. Their earlier prediction, at the Primates' Meeting at Lambeth Palace in 2003, that rejection of the faith committed to us would 'tear the fabric of our Communion at its deepest level', has proved to be accurate. In Dar es Salaam the Primates proposed, as one last attempt to restore unity, that there should be a period of seven months, during which those who had brought our Communion to the brink of destruction should reconsider their actions, and put a stop to the harmful actions that have so polarized our beloved church.

The Primates set a deadline, 30 September 2007, for receiving an answer. This deadline was ignored.

There is no longer any hope, therefore, for a unified Communion. The intransigence of those who reject Biblical authority continues to obstruct our mission, and it now seems that the Communion is being forced to choose between following their innovations or continuing on the path that the Church has followed since the time of the Apostles. We have made enormous efforts since 1997 in seeking to avoid this crisis, but without success. Now we confront a moment of decision. If we fail to act, we risk leading millions of people away from the faith revealed in the Holy Scriptures and also, even more seriously, we face the real possibility of denying our Saviour, the Lord Jesus Christ.

The leadership of The Episcopal Church USA (ECUSA) and the Anglican Church of Canada (ACoC) seem to have concluded that the Bible is no longer authoritative in many areas of human experience, especially those of salvation and sexuality. They claim to have 'progressed' beyond the clear teaching of the Scriptures, and they have not hidden their intention of leading others to these same conclusions. They have even boasted that they are years ahead of others in fully understanding the truth of the Holy Scriptures and the nature of God's love.

Both ECUSA and ACoC have been given several opportunities to consult, discuss and prayerfully respond, through their recognized structures. By way of response they have produced carefully nuanced, deliberately ambiguous statements, but their actions have betrayed these statements. Their intention is clear; they have chosen to walk away from the biblically-based path we once all walked together. And the unrelenting persecution, of those among them who remain faithful, shows how they have used these past few years to isolate and destroy any and all opposition.

We now confront the seriousness of their actions, as the time for the Lambeth Conference draws near. Sadly, this Conference has not been designed, as in the past, as an opportunity for serious theological engagement and heartfelt reconciliation. We are told that it will be a time of prayer, fellowship and communion. These are commendable activities, but this very Communion has already been broken by the actions of the American and Canadian Churches. The consequence is most serious, for if even a single province chooses not to attend, the Lambeth Conference effectively ceases to be an Instrument of Unity. Moreover, the status of the Archbishop of Canterbury, as convenor and as an instrument or focus of unity, also becomes highly questionable.

Repentance and reversal by these North American provinces may yet save our Communion. Failure to recognize the gravity of this moment will have a devastating impact.

1. *Scorned opportunities*

Following the 1997 warning, the 1998 Lambeth Conference issued Resolution 1.10. This affirmed the teaching of the Holy Scriptures with regard to faithfulness in marriage between a man and a woman in lifelong union, and declared that homosexual practice was incompatible with Biblical teaching. Then, in March 2000, at their meeting in Oporto, Portugal, the Primates reaffirmed the supremacy of Scripture as the 'decisive authority in the life of our Communion'.

However, in July 2000 the General Convention of the Episcopal Church USA responded by approving Resolution D039, which acknowledged relationships other than marriage 'in the Body of Christ and in this Church', and stated that those 'who disagree with the traditional teaching of the Church on human sexuality, will act in contradiction to that position'!

The Convention only narrowly avoided directing the Standing Commission on Liturgy and Music to begin preparation of official rites for the blessing of 'these relationships ... other than marriage'.

In 2001, the Primates' Meeting in Kanuga, North Carolina, issued a pastoral letter acknowledging estrangement in the Church, due to changes in theology and practice regarding human sexuality, and calling on all provinces of the Communion to avoid actions that might damage the 'credibility of mission in the world'. In April 2002, after their meeting at Canterbury, the Primates issued a further pastoral letter, recognizing the responsibility of all bishops to articulate the fundamentals of faith and maintain Christian truth.

In what appeared to be an act of deliberate defiance, the Diocese of New Westminster in Canada voted, in June 2002, to approve the blessing of same-sex unions, with the enthusiastic support of their bishop, Michael Ingham. Later that year the twelfth meeting of the Anglican Consultative Council took place in October, in Hong Kong, and a resolution [34] was approved that urged dioceses and bishops to refrain from unilateral actions and policies that would strain communion.

The following year, however, when ECUSA met in General Convention in Minneapolis in July/August, they chose, among their many actions, to reject a Resolution [B001] that affirmed the authority of Scripture and other basic elements of Christian faith. They also approved the election as bishop [C045] of someone living in an unashamedly sexual relationship outside marriage.

The Primates' Meeting specially convened at Lambeth Palace, in October 2003, issued a pastoral statement condemning ECUSA's decisions at General Convention, describing them as actions that 'threaten the unity of our own Communion as well as our relationships with other parts of Christ's Church, our mission and witness, and our relations with other faiths, in a world already confused in areas of sexuality, morality and theology and polarized Christian opinion.' They also declared that if the consecration proceeded 'the future of the Communion itself will be put in jeopardy', and that the action would 'tear the fabric of our communion at its deepest level, and may lead to further division on this and further issues as provinces have to decide in consequence whether they can remain in communion with provinces that choose not to break communion with the Episcopal Church (USA)'. They also called on 'the provinces concerned to make adequate provision for Episcopal oversight of dissenting minorities within their own area of pastoral care in consultation with the Archbishop of Canterbury on behalf of the Primates'. ECUSA responded, the following month, by proceeding with the consecration of Gene Robinson, thereby tearing the fabric of our Communion and forcing the Church of Nigeria, along with many other provinces, to sever communion with ECUSA.

Earlier, in June 2003, we in the Church of Nigeria had cut our links with the diocese of New Westminster, and sent a clear warning about the reconsidering of our relationship with ECUSA, should Gene Robinson be consecrated. As always, we were ignored.

During 2004 there was a growing number of so-called 'blessings' of same-sex unions by American and Canadian priests, even though The Windsor Report, released in September 2004, reaffirmed Lambeth Resolution 1.10, and also the authority of Scripture as being central to Anglican Common Life. The Windsor Report also called for two moratoria, one on public rites of same-sex blessing, and the other on the election to the episcopate, and consent, of any candidate who was living in a same-sex union.

One consequence of this continuing intransigence by ECUSA was the alienation of thousands of faithful Anglicans who make their home in the USA. The attempts by the Primates to provide for their protection, through the Panel of

Reference, proved fruitless. So, the desire of these faithful Anglicans for an alternative spiritual home led to many impassioned requests to the Church of Nigeria, and also to a number of other provinces within the Global South. The Standing Committee of the Church of Nigeria recognized this urgent need during their meeting in Ilesa in March 2004 and, as a result, initiated a process for the provision of pastoral care through the formation of a Convocation within the USA.

The Province of Nigeria made the conscious decision to initiate the Convocation of Anglicans in North America (CANA) in the light of the following:

- the undisputed alienation among Anglicans in North America created by the actions of ECUSA, despite warnings from the Instruments of Communion.

- the need for pastoral care and oversight for alienated Anglicans in North America in the light of the Primates Communiqué in October 2003. 'The provinces concerned to make adequate provision for episcopal oversight of dissenting minorities within their own area of pastoral care in consultation with the Archbishop of Canterbury on behalf of the Primates.'

- ECUSA's establishment of Churches in the diocese of Europe.

- The consecration and appointment of Bishop Sandy Millar as a bishop of the Province of Uganda, called to serve in the United Kingdom.

As a matter of courtesy, the Archbishop of Canterbury was duly informed of our intentions.

During the African Anglican Bishops Conference (AABC), in October 2004, the Primates who were present released a statement which, among other things, urged the

Episcopal Church USA and the Anglican Church of Canada to take seriously the need for 'repentance, forgiveness and reconciliation enjoined on all Christians by Christ'. It called on these two Churches to move beyond informal expressions of regret for the effect of their actions, and to have a genuine change of heart and mind.

Although, at their meeting in The Dromantine, Northern Ireland in February 2005, the Primates advised the withdrawal of both ECUSA and the ACoC from the Anglican Consultative Council, the continued influence of these Churches on the Communion, and their renewed efforts to cause others to adopt their intransigent line, frustrated any genuine attempts at reconciliation. The agonizing journey towards unity and faith seemed unending.

The obvious reluctance of the Archbishop of Canterbury, and the unwillingness of the other Instruments of Unity, to effect discipline on those who had rejected the mind of the Communion, prompted the Church of Nigeria to effect a change in her constitution, during a General Synod held in Onitsha in September 2005. This constitutional change not only protects the Church of Nigeria from being led into error by any Church in the Communion, but also makes full constitutional provision for the Convocation of Anglicans in North America (CANA).

The Third Anglican South-to-South Encounter, meeting in Egypt in October 2005, issued a very strong indictment of ECUSA and the ACoC, and called for a common 'Anglican Covenant' among Churches remaining true to Biblical Christianity and historic Anglicanism.

Despite all the calls for repentance, the blessing of homosexual unions, and the nominating of practising homosexuals to the episcopacy, continued in the USA, with the Archbishop of Canterbury expressing 'deep unease' with such nominations in California in February 2006. (An article describing the reaction of the Archbishop of Canterbury, Archbishop Rowan Williams, to the California election is to be found in the Church of England Newspaper, February 24th, 2006.)

The much-awaited ECUSA General Convention in 2006 proved to be a disappointment: resolutions expressing regret for the harm done to the communion were rejected, as was one that tried to emphasize the necessity of Christ for salvation. Among the resolutions that were approved was one promoting homosexual relationships, and another that apologized to homosexuals for the following of Biblical principles by the Anglican Communion. A pledge to include openly homosexual persons was requested 'of our sister churches in the Anglican Communion and Anglican Communion bodies as evidence of the apology'. Finally, someone who does not regard homosexual behaviour a sin, and who does not consider Jesus to be the only way to the Father, was elected as Presiding Bishop. The agony of a frustrated Communion was visible worldwide, except among those already prepared to embrace this dangerous path of departing from the faith.

The Church of Nigeria needed no further prodding to proceed with the election, in June 2006, and then in August 2006 the consecration, of the Rt. Rev. Martyn Minns, to give Episcopal oversight to CANA. The Nigerian House of Bishops also declared a reluctance to participate in the 2008 Lambeth Conference with an unrepentant ECUSA and Anglican Church of Canada. (The Minutes of the Church of Nigeria's House of Bishops' meeting, in June 2006, confirm this.)

The Global South Anglican Primates, meeting in Kigali in September 2006, recognized that ECUSA appeared to have no intention of changing direction and once again embracing the 'faith once delivered'. In their communiqué they wrote: 'We are convinced that the time has now come to take initial steps towards the formation of what will be recognized as a separate ecclesiastical structure of the Anglican Communion in the USA ... We believe that we would be failing in our apostolic witness if we do not make this provision for those who hold firmly to a commitment to historic Anglican faith.'

The Anglican Communion Primates, meeting in Dar es Salaam in February 2007, reaffirmed the 1998 Lambeth Resolution 1:10 and called on ECUSA (now renamed The Episcopal Church, TEC) to consider definite actions, which could heal the Communion as well as reassure those who had been deprived of adequate pastoral care. The Primates had set a deadline of 30 September, by which date they hoped to have a response. By June 2007, both the ACoC and TEC had indicated an unwillingness to comply with these requests, but had expressed a desire to remain part of the Communion they had hurt so much. The Primates' deadline came, and went; it was ignored. The situation had been made even more incoherent by the decision, made earlier in the year, to extend an invitation to the Lambeth Conference to those responsible for this crisis, with no accompanying call to repentance, but not to invite certain bishops, such as Bishop Martyn Minns, who have stood firm for the Faith. And so, now, we fail to see how these two positions can ever be reconciled.

2.   All journeys must end some day

Therefore, since we are surrounded by such a great cloud of witnesses, let us throw off everything that hinders and the sin that so easily entangles, and let us run with perseverance the race marked out for us. (Hebrews 12:1)

These past ten years of distraction have been agonizing, and the cost has been enormous. The time and financial resources spent on endless meetings, whose statements and warnings have been consistently ignored, represent a tragic loss of resources that should have been used otherwise. It now appears, however, that the journey is coming to an end, and the moment of decision is almost upon us. But this is not a time to lose heart or fail to maintain vigilance. It would be an even greater tragedy if, while trying to bring others back to the godly path, we should ourselves miss the way or lose the race.

- We want unity, but not at the cost of relegating Christ to the position of another 'wise teacher' who can be obeyed or disobeyed.

- We earnestly desire the healing of our beloved Communion, but not at the cost of re-writing the Bible to accommodate the latest cultural trend.

As stated in *The Road to Lambeth*: 'We Anglicans stand at a crossroads. One road, the road of compromise of biblical truth, leads to destruction and disunity. The other road has its own obstacles [faithfulness is never an easy way] because it requires changes in the way the Communion has been governed and it challenges [all] our churches to live up to and into their full maturity in Christ.'

The first road, the one that follows the current path of The Episcopal Church USA and the Anglican Church of Canada, is one that we simply cannot take: the cost is too high. We must not sacrifice eternal truth for mere

---

1   http://www.globalsouthanglican.org/index.php/comments/the_road_to_lambeth_presented_at_capa/

appeasement, and we must not turn away from the source of life and love for the sake of a temporary truce.

The other road is the only one that we can embrace. It is not an easy road because it demands obedience and faithfulness from each one of us. It requires an unequivocal acceptance of, and commitment to:

- the authority and supremacy of Scripture

- the doctrine of the Trinity

- the person, work and resurrection of Jesus the Christ

- the acknowledgement of Jesus as divine, and the one and only means of salvation

- the biblical teaching on sin, forgiveness, reconciliation, and transformation by the Holy Spirit through Christ

- the sanctity of marriage

- teaching about morality that is rooted and grounded in biblical revelation

- apostolic ministry

These are not onerous burdens or tiresome restrictions, but rather they are God's gift, designed to set us free from the bondage of sin and give us the assurance of life eternal.

It is our hope and fervent prayer that, in the coming months, all those in leadership will be directed towards the restoration of true unity in the Body of Christ, by means of an unconditional embrace of the One who says to all who will listen, 'If you love me, you will obey what I command.'

John Bunyan, the author of *The Pilgrim's Progress*, describes the Christian life as a journey from the City of Destruction to the Celestial City. On his journey, numerous decisions and many crossroads confront Christian, the pilgrim. The easy road was never the right road. In the same way, we have arrived at a crossroads; it is, for us, the moment of truth.

This day I call heaven and earth as witnesses against you that I have set before you life and death, blessings and curses. Now choose life, so that you and your children may live and that you may love the LORD your God, listen to his voice, and hold fast to him. (Deuteronomy 30:19,20a)

Authentic Anglicanism

And Jesus came and said to them, 'All authority in heaven and on earth has been given to me. Go therefore and make disciples of all nations, baptizing them in the name of the Father and of the Son and of the Holy Spirit, teaching them to observe all that I have commanded you. And behold, I am with you always, to the end of the age.' (Matt. 28:18–20)

'The times of ignorance God overlooked, but now he commands all people everywhere to repent, because he has fixed a day on which he will judge the world in righteousness by a man whom he has appointed; and of this he has given assurance to all by raising him from the dead.' (Acts 17:30–31)

The all-encompassing Lordship of Christ, the certainty that God's purposes will be fulfilled, and the urgency of Christian mission in the last days – these are the foundational elements which provide both the context and the content of our future as Anglican Christians. This future calls for a renewed determination, on our part, to submit all our thoughts, actions and plans to the scrutiny of God's word, with humble and repentant hearts.

We rejoice in the grace and mercy of the living God, in our identity as disciples of his Christ, and in the heritage of authentic Anglicanism that we have received from those faithful men and women who have gone before us. We rejoice in the presence of God among his people today as, through his word and by his Spirit, he enables us to live before him, and in the world, as men and women being conformed to the likeness of Christ, and committed to proclaiming the salvation that he has won for all who come to him in faith.

Authentic Anglicanism is a particular expression of Christian corporate life which seeks to honour the Lord Jesus Christ by nurturing faith, and also encouraging obedience to the teaching of God's written word, meaning the canonical Scriptures of the Old and New Testaments. It embraces the Thirty-nine Articles of Religion (published in the year 1571) and the Book of Common Prayer (the two versions of 1552 and 1662), both texts being read according to their plain and historical sense, and being accepted as faithful expressions of the teaching of Scripture, which provides the standard for Anglican theology and practice.

While authentic Anglicanism makes no claim to be perfect, and respects Christians of other traditions, it nevertheless insists on certain basic theological commitments. These are to be found in the classic documents of the Anglican tradition, but they need to be reiterated and reaffirmed in each generation. The non-negotiable core of these commitments includes:

- the goodness, love and mercy of the living God who eternally exists in three Persons, Father, Son and Holy Spirit;

- the creation of men and women by God in his image, with all that this means for the dignity and value of every human life;

- the distortion of creation, at all levels, by the decision of the first man and woman to turn aside from trust in God's goodness, expressed in the word he had given them;

- the lostness of the human race, as the result of the fall into sin, which manifests itself in our natural guilt, corruption and enslavement to sinful desire;

- the uniqueness of Jesus Christ as the incarnate Son of God, and as the only Saviour for sinful men and women;

- the central saving reality of judgement being borne in our place by Jesus Christ on the cross, which is his great victory over all that stands against us, and that also stands opposed to the rightful rule of God;

- the historical actuality and theological indispensability of the bodily resurrection of Jesus Christ from the dead, on the third day after his crucifixion, leaving empty the tomb in which he had been laid;

- the necessity of the Spirit's work in bringing about repentance and faith in the human heart, so as to unite us to Christ and enable us to share in the salvation he has won;

- the right standing with God which is given freely, and which now belongs to all who, by faith, are united to Jesus Christ in his death and resurrection;

- the expectation of the bodily return of Jesus Christ, to bring God's purposes of salvation and judgement to their consummation;

- the significance of the Church as the gathering of the redeemed people of God around the word of God and in the Spirit of God;

- the supreme authority of the Scriptures as the word of God written, and as the source of true teaching about God, his purposes, and the appropriate response to God's mercy in Jesus Christ;

- the purpose of Christian ministry within the churches to nourish faith and obedience through careful teaching of the Bible in the context of genuine personal relationships;

- the generous provision of the Lord's Supper and baptism which, as sacraments, visibly represent the promises of the gospel of Jesus Christ to his people;

- the legitimate exercise of authority within the churches which is characterized by unreserved obedience to the teaching of Scripture and Jesus Christ's own pattern of service;

- the importance of fellowship between Christian congregations in the common cause of living as disciples of Jesus Christ and as his ambassadors in the world;

- the priority of evangelism for all Christians in response to the great commission of Jesus Christ.

What is at stake?

The Anglican Communion has been proud of its comprehensiveness. In recent times, however, some parts of the Communion have been allowed to develop in such a way that their expressions of faith and life, now, can hardly be recognized as being Christian, let alone being Anglican. There are five areas in which we perceive that what has been entrusted to the Church is currently under threat. They are areas, therefore, that are being fiercely contested.

1. *The struggle over authority, for the Church and for the Christian*

Your word is a lamp to my feet and a light to my path. (Psalm 119:105)

1.1. The nature of divine revelation, and the nature of the text of the Bible – these are the prime matters being disputed.

All Anglicans agree, formally, that the Bible has supreme authority. But what is the nature of this authority? Is the authority tied to the Biblical text, or does it operate independently of it? Or is this authority expressed through a variety of texts, persons and institutions?

We begin with the possibility of our recognizing and receiving God's revelation, in spite of our fallen nature. The Fall adversely affected, but has not destroyed, human ability to recognize and receive God's revelation. For God created us for fellowship with himself. Also, importantly, God himself links the revelation with the text through his Holy Spirit, who 'breathes' the text.

1.2. All Anglicans agree that ultimate authority lies in God alone. The question is, how does he exercise his authority? And how are we to understand the way he acts? Are we to say that he acts in the same way as, and alongside, other actors and agents?

God's authority is not abstract. It is expressed through human persons and institutions, including the family, the Church and the community of the chosen people. Since God links his authority to his words, as given in Scripture, the Biblical text possesses a privileged status, in relation to human persons and institutions, precisely because it contains God's words, given and brought home to the human heart by the living activity of his Holy Spirit.

1.3. How should we understand revelation? It is the presence of God, and it is also God speaking to his people. These two understandings are completely compatible; they are only falsely opposed to one another. God exercises his authority through his Spirit, by means of the words which he addresses to particular human beings. Those who disagree with this claim will ask whether that speech is episodic and time-bound, as would be suggested by its expression in a historical text, or whether it is of a different order from human-to-human speech. It cannot be correct, however, that God's words might be time-bound, for if that were the case the incarnation would be marginalised. The highest expression of divine speech is the Word made flesh, who was with God from the beginning, and who upholds all things by his word of power. In addition, the New Testament writers recognize the Scriptures as being God's speech to us now – the writer to the Hebrews, for example, stresses this in chapters three and four of his epistle. They do not view the Scriptures as a reduced form of communication, or an echo of a word spoken in the past, or as merely a background against which we hope to discern what God is saying to us today.

To take the Bible seriously is to take seriously the one who communicated its words. It should not be supposed, however, that recognizing the Bible as God's speech is idolatry. We realize, and acknowledge, that we are under the authority of the Bible, and we expect the word to confront us with new and even strange things. We do not become masters of the word. And God does not reinforce our prejudices!

We are not free to pick and choose in Scripture. All of it is God's revelation, and all of it needs to be taken seriously.

2. *The struggle over the interpretation of Scripture*

The above view of authority carries with it several implications for the interpretation of Scripture.

2.1. While some say that the meaning of Scripture is so complex, and so contested, that it cannot be fixed, we argue that the heart of Scripture is plain, even though some parts are not simple. It is plain enough to call forth our faith and obedience, which together lead us to further understanding of the Bible's meaning. It is plain enough to be the basis on which we make a stand.

2.2. Another element in this struggle is the distinction that is sometimes made between the main teachings of the Bible and the lesser ones, those that are referred to as *adiaphora*, meaning 'things that are indifferent'. According to this view, some doctrinal and moral issues may be put aside because they do not really matter, while others must be affirmed by all. This distinction is seen as essential for the unity of the church, and yet the Bible itself never applies it in this way. And in Anglican tradition *adiaphora* are primarily matters to do with ceremonies and robes, and not issues concerning doctrine or morality.

2.3. How are Christians to ensure that their understanding, or interpretation, of Scripture is valid? The historic pattern is that the Church arrives at one mind after meeting together, and deliberating, in Council. It takes care to establish that its decisions are faithful to the teaching of Scripture, and that they stand in continuity with the Church's life and message through the centuries. The Church also seeks to make provision for Christians to test these decisions against the Scriptures, according to the example of the Berean Christians who 'examined the Scriptures daily' (Acts 17:10-12). This is the true meaning of the technical term 'reception'. In the current climate, however, there is often a tension between those who seek a deeper understanding of what has already been given, in Scripture, for example the meaning of God's provision of marriage and family, and those who claim that they have received a new revelation, for example that same-sex activity is holy.

3. The struggle over theological pluralism in the Church

3.1. The Anglican Church has always been a confessional institution, but its confession does not seek to be comprehensive on every issue, or to foreclose discussion. Over the last two hundred years, however, an unwillingness has grown up, in some parts of the Church, to bind itself to confessional formulae, such as the Thirty-nine Articles. Instead, there has been a strong move towards a more general affirmation of the Thirty-nine Articles, accepting them as a historical background which informs our life and witness, but not as a test of faith. As long as this unwillingness remains, there is little hope for an effective Covenant within the Anglican Communion.

3.2. Liberal Anglican leaders and theologians insist, in their rhetoric, upon the comprehensiveness of the Church, but in reality they have problems with a comprehensiveness that includes the orthodox. Comprehensiveness, hitherto, has been maintained by a liberal consensus in which liberals defined the space, setting its boundaries, and provided legitimacy for every section of the Church. This has now broken down.[2] The liberal consensus turned from transcendent realities, about which there was religious dispute, to the reality of the world, which all could supposedly agree on. But this reality is seen to be riven with discord, and in that discord liberals have now taken the side of the victim, and no longer claim universal representation. Since, therefore, liberals in places of power have now insisted on entrenching their views and excluding those who disagree, conservatives are unwilling to be confined to the marginal space assigned to them, and realize that they do not need the liberal establishment for legitimacy.

3.3. The liberals focus on shared worship, shared work and shared experience, but not on shared faith. In contrast, the New Testament concept of fellowship is anchored in a common faith and a common mind (Phil. 2:1-2; 1 John 1:1-3).

4.   *The struggle over the understanding of mission*

4.1. The Anglican Church is committed to proclaiming the gospel of Jesus Christ crucified and risen. For some, however, the Church is itself the message. By this they mean that the Anglican Church's own diversity, and its ability to live with plurality and contradiction in its own membership on matters of faith, is precisely the witness it gives to a plural society today.

But the Bible teaches that the Church Christ founded is

---

2   See Professor Oliver O'Donovan's sermons at http://www.fulcrum-anglican.org.uk/news/2006/20060703odonovan1.cfm?doc=122

entrusted with a message, and that its members are to be transformed by this message. Paul's teaching, on the relativising of different identities, and on their restoration in Christ, is clear. In the Church of Christ different identities (of race, nationality, class, gender) are not merely included, they are transformed. And they are relativised by being included in the identity of the crucified and risen Lord. They then bear one message: the good news of Christ's death and resurrection, and his transforming power. Christians do not simply belong to a message, they bear that message in their lives.

4.2. Anglican mission has always taken seriously the culture of the diverse peoples in which the gospel is expressed and lived out. At the same time, it has always seen the gospel message as being translatable into any culture, without any fear that its universality might be compromised. This is at the heart of the Anglican Reformation. So, at any time or in any place, the church is both catholic, belonging to the universal church, and part of a particular culture. But because of the givenness of Scripture and the catholicity of the faith, and because the church is the bearer of a transcendent and transforming gospel, it has always been called to confront human cultures, rather than adapt itself to them. A recent example of this was when the Church in Kenya confronted the political rulers, whose traditional expectations were to maintain their own dominance through unjust means, with the clear teaching of the Scriptures.

4.3. The contemporary tendency to disconnect belief from behaviour affects the Anglican Church today very significantly. The secular view is that behaviour is primarily a personal matter; it cannot be imposed. This means that the belief on which a person bases his or her behaviour is also a personal matter. But Biblical teaching calls for behaviour which is compatible with the teaching of Scripture.

Human sinfulness and selfishness easily find rationalisations for chosen behaviours, even behaviours that are clearly contrary to the plain teaching of Scripture. In our day the privatisation of belief, and the perceived need for the expression of individual authenticity, mean that any imposition of behaviour from outside will be rejected. There is no room, however, for such views in a Biblically faithful Christian church.

4.4. Contemporary cultures increasingly place Eros, human love, at the centre of human authenticity and fulfilment. It is here that orthodox Christians need to struggle to recover a Biblical understanding of human love, as being both profoundly natural and transcendent. In Biblical teaching, human love, if it is to be meaningful, satisfying and transcendent, must be expressed in the order that God has provided, in a faithful, monogamous heterosexual relationship. Every other expression, particularly of sexual love, is seen in Scripture as destructive, both of the family, the order that God gives for human flourishing, and of the individual's own wellbeing. For this reason it is forbidden.

4.5. The writings of the Bible emerged in contexts of religious plurality. But the challenge to the people of God was to share the uniqueness of their God in such a context. This challenge still stands, in a world of increasing religious pluralism.

5. *The struggle over post-colonial power relationships*

The issue of Anglican identity is affected by these matters:

5.1. The question of legitimation: Who defines Anglicanism? Who legitimizes the brand?

5.2. Geography: Globalisation has made geographical boundaries irrelevant in most areas of life. People's attachments and identities are no longer primarily geographical. It is this that must now shape the way in which fellowship and accountability are experienced in the Anglican Communion.

5.3. Power and post-colonial realities: The Anglican Communion has yet to face up to the reality of post-colonial Anglicanism, not just in terms of national Churches in the non-Western world, but in terms of Churches with increasing numbers, and the power that attends such growth. There is an analogy with the rise of China and India in the global economic world. The rest of the world seeks to adjust and relate effectively to such realities. In Anglicanism, however, the rise is resisted vigorously by some sections, while others embrace it uncritically. The Church, as the first Global Community, is called to demonstrate a way of dealing with power and accountability that witnesses to the transforming power of the risen Lord.

In conclusion – the struggle today is to affirm that the plain truth is accessible to the ordinary person. Those who deny that this is possible then define everything in terms of power, in a situation in which they hold the upper hand and their power is being challenged by this very appeal to truth. Repeated attempts at dialogue have been made by those committed to the teaching of Scripture. However, experience has shown that the revisionists are not willing to listen.

We now turn to examine four issues in greater detail:

1. the nature of Anglican orthodoxy, and thus the nature of Anglican identity;

2. the implications of the confession that Jesus is Lord, in the Church and in mission;

3. how the authority of Jesus is to be expressed and obeyed, and

4. how we are to worship God.

Finally, we look forward to our journey into the future.

1.   Anglican orthodoxy

1.1.   *Anglican orthodoxy defined*

The phrase 'Anglican orthodoxy' may sound strange to some ears. Anglicanism, despite many contacts with the Eastern Orthodox Churches, has never been in communion with them, nor pretended to be Orthodox in the way that they are. Of course 'orthodoxy' is no more the exclusive domain of the Eastern Churches than 'catholicity' is of Rome. Nevertheless, the current use of the term among conservative Anglicans calls for some explanation.

In its basic sense, orthodoxy means 'holding correct doctrine' or, to use a phrase from the East African Revival, 'walking in the light', as opposed to 'walking in darkness' (1 John 1:6-7), which is 'heresy'. The concern for Christian orthodoxy goes back to the time of the apostles. In the later Epistles, the theme of sound doctrine being attacked by false teaching is particularly apparent.

- St. Paul describes the responsibility of a bishop in this way: 'He must hold firm to the doctrine (*didache*) of the faithful word, so that he may be able to expound sound doctrine (*didaskalia*) and confute those who contradict it' (Titus 1:9).

- For St. John, holding true teaching will include a person in the love of God, but holding false teaching will exclude a person from his love: 'Any one who goes ahead and does not abide in the doctrine of Christ does not have God; he who abides in the doctrine has both the Father and the Son' (2 John 9). Indeed, the division between orthodoxy and heresy has serious communal implications, as seen in John's command which follows: 'If any one comes to you and does not bring this doctrine, do not receive him into the house or give him any greeting' (2 John 10).

- Similarly, St. Jude, the Lord's brother, writes to the Church, 'appealing to you to contend for the faith which was once for all delivered to the saints' (Jude 3). Jude makes it clear that the particular heresy plaguing the Church has to do with moral teachings from 'ungodly persons who pervert the grace of our God into licentiousness and deny our only Master and Lord, Jesus Christ' (verse 4).

From this apostolic teaching the 'rule of faith', or 'rule of truth', was derived. It was on the basis of this that the early Church opposed various heresies, such as Marcionism, Gnosticism and Arianism. The rule was elaborated by the early Councils, whose decisions became creedal for later generations of catholic and orthodox Christians.

Although the Reformation of the sixteenth century burst forth with a new vitality and new learning in many areas, its fundamental claim was that it represented a continuation of, and indeed a return to, the original apostolic faith. Anglican apologists like Bishop John Jewell argued that 'the catholic fathers and bishops made no doubt but that our religion might be proved out of the Holy Scriptures. Neither were they ever so hardy to take any for an heretic whose error they could not evidently and apparently reprove by the self-same Scriptures.' (*Apology*, pp.19-20).

One of the Thirty-nine Articles of Religion notes that the Churches of Jerusalem, Alexandria, Antioch and Rome have erred in matters of faith, morals and ceremonies (Article XIX). This implies that 'orthodoxy' cannot be equated with any one Church or tradition. Instead, it must be proved by Holy Scripture (Article VI). Though the Articles focused on what Scripture reveals concerning those things necessary for salvation, their author, Archbishop Thomas Cranmer, intended that they should also be confessional. Clergy in the Church of England were expected to affirm them 'from the heart' (*ex animo*), and some Churches today (e.g., Nigeria) continue this practice. This standard of orthodoxy is upheld by the Anglican Ordinal, in which two key vows are required of priests and bishops: 'Are you persuaded that the holy Scriptures contain sufficiently all doctrine required of necessity for eternal salvation through faith in Jesus Christ?', and 'Will you be ready, with all faithful diligence, to banish and drive away all erroneous and strange doctrines contrary to God's Word ...?'

The universal acceptance of the Prayer Book and the Articles, as standards of Anglican teaching, seemed to guarantee Biblical orthodoxy, but, like the Church in Ephesus (Revelation 2:1-7), Anglicanism suffered from latitudinarian indifference rather than overt heresy. The regulatory force of the Articles was weakened, from the late seventeenth century, and replaced with a rationalistic moralism. By the mid-nineteenth century, concerns began to arise that the Church of England was no longer ruled by the plain sense of Scripture and its classic formularies. One challenge came from John Henry Newman and the Tractarians, who reinterpreted the Articles in a Roman direction. From the liberal side, Bishop Colenso of Natal was seen to employ 'higher criticism' of the Bible in order to question the authority of Scripture. This latter challenge led to the calling of the first Lambeth Conference. The Lambeth Quadrilateral, adopted at the third Conference, functioned as a means of steering a middle course through the modernist-catholic debates, while promoting a basis for ecumenical dialogue. Some have seen the Quadrilateral as an adequate definition of Anglican orthodoxy, but the current crisis has shown that, without the recovery across the Communion of the classic doctrinal and liturgical formularies, it is inadequate to the task.

The growing strength of liberalism, however, undermined hopes for a renewed orthodox consensus. In particular, English and American Anglicanism fell victim to certain bishops – John A.T. Robinson and David Jenkins on one side of the Atlantic, and James Pike and John Spong on the other – who questioned the very 'substance' of orthodox Christianity: the transcendence of God, the possibility of miracles, the Virgin Birth and Bodily Resurrection of Christ and, underlying all, the authority of the Bible. These bishops kept their office and were, at most, lightly rapped over the knuckles for their controversial views. In the case of The Episcopal Church USA (TEC), such 'prophetic' views were stamped as mainstream with the election of Katherine Jefferts Schori as Presiding Bishop in 2006. Increasingly, the words 'Anglicanism' and 'crisis' began appearing in the same sentence.

At the very time that Western Anglicanism was drifting from the orthodox faith, new movements of Anglicanism were arising in the so-called Global South. Rooted in the nineteenth-century Evangelical and Anglo-Catholic missions, African, Asian and South American Anglicanism became indigenous, part of a wider movement which Philip Jenkins has labelled, rather dramatically, *The Next Christendom*. The Anglican Church of Nigeria, for instance, took Lambeth 1988's 'Decade of Evangelism' to heart, and planted churches that increased its membership from 14 million people to 18 million. (This growth has continued into a second decade, so that Nigerian Anglicans now number about 20 million.)

Anglicans in the Global South were at first surprised, and then appalled, to learn of the promotion of homosexuality by the Churches in the West. While some of their abhorrence may be rooted in their culture, much of it derives from their reverence for Scripture. 'The missionaries brought us this book,' one African bishop said at Lambeth in 1998, 'and we are not going to turn our backs on it.' Some of these Anglicans see themselves in a spiritual battle: 'the acts of God versus the acts of Satan', as one Nigerian theologian put it. These Anglicans have now forged alliances with orthodox Anglicans in Western churches such as TEC, the Anglican Church of Canada and the Church of England itself. Though they may be divided as to how to respond to the weak leadership of the Anglican Communion since 1998, the Global South Churches are united in their commitment to Biblical authority and Anglican orthodoxy.

Whether spelled out by the 2008 Lambeth Conference, in terms of an Anglican Covenant, or evidenced by the convening of the Global Anglican Future Conference (GAFCON), it is clear that there is a need to explore and define anew, for Anglicans worldwide, what it means to be orthodox, and also how they should respond to those who transgress into the territory of heresy.

1.2. *Anglican orthodoxy in a global context today*

The Articles of Religion, in distinguishing the Biblical essentials of salvation from those other matters which may be affected by time and culture, open up the possibility of a significant diversity in orthodox Anglican piety and polity. The typology of three streams of Anglican faith and practice – evangelical, catholic and charismatic – has been widely observed for more than thirty years, especially since the advent of charismatic movements inside the church. Such a typology is easily caricatured and easily misunderstood, like the image of Anglicanism as a three-legged stool (Scripture, tradition and reason). But there is legitimate value in the three-streams model, especially when they are seen as flowing together into one river – no doubt with different currents and eddies. The value of this typology is also enhanced when it is removed from the historical polemics in the Western Churches and applied to the Global South Churches and the wider mission field.

1.2.1. *Evangelical*

Anglican orthodoxy is, first and foremost, *evangelical*. The Gospel of salvation through Jesus Christ – preached, believed and defended, is at the heart of the apostolic message. Evangelical Christianity is necessarily triune in shape: John Stott defines evangelical priorities as 'the revealing initiative of God the Father, the redeeming work of God the Son and the transforming ministry of God the Holy Spirit' (*Evangelical Truth*, p.25).

The Gospel is conveyed through God's word written in Scripture, and preached by pastors from the pulpit and evangelists on the street corner. In the words of the famous hymn,

> The church from her dear Master
> Received the gift divine,
> And still the light she lifteth
> O'er all the earth to shine.
> It is the golden casket
> Where gems of truth are stored;
> It is the heav'n-drawn picture
> Of Christ, the living Word.[3]

Though Islam claims to possess the final word from God, this word may only be read in Arabic. By contrast, Anglican missionaries laboured to translate the Bible and the Prayer

---

3   'O Word of God Incarnate' by William W. How, 1823-1897

Book into the vernacular, and converts were known as 'readers'. Historically, the church has taken the lead in promoting formal education, in all parts of the world, and even today has been involved in founding new universities in East Africa.

The Gospel is worth fighting for and dying for. The preaching of the Gospel and its defence in the face of paganism and heresy are God-ordained activities, for all Christians at all times. At the time of the Reformation, Martin Luther's cry – 'Here I stand, I can do no other!' – epitomized the stance of the primitive Church. And over the centuries the noble army of martyrs, those known and unknown individuals 'whose voice cries out', has included countless Anglicans, from the martyrs of Oxford and Uganda to the many in modern times who have lost their lives in Islamic regions.

Besides its emphasis on the Gospel, Evangelical Anglicanism has another side: a spirit of liberality. It may seem strange to include 'liberality' alongside *sola scriptura*, the gifts of the Spirit and the cost of discipleship, but it should not be. As St. Paul says, '... where the Spirit is, there is liberty.' (2 Corinthians 3:17), and his own pastoral practice as an apostle exemplifies the aphorism: 'In essentials, unity; in non-essentials, liberty; in all things, charity.' Liberality of spirit characterizes the Anglican *via media* approach to doctrinal, liturgical and pastoral matters, which seeks to be firm in matters of salvation and modest with regard to secondary or 'indifferent' matters (*adiaphora*). Going back to John Jewell and Richard Hooker, this 'sweet reasonableness' (Titus 3:2) has been a hallmark of Anglican writers, with George Herbert, C. S. Lewis and John Stott being prime examples.

Though it may be a virtue in secondary matters, tolerance can and does lead to an opposite vice: spiritual laxity, which manifests itself in pastoral laziness and doctrinal slovenliness. In *The Great Divorce,* C. S. Lewis was quick to point out the perversion of liberality, in his portrait of an Anglican bishop who says, 'There is no such thing as a final answer ... to travel hopefully is better than to arrive.' Such smug mediocrity, evident today in the Anglican Communion's turmoil, has led some African church leaders to invoke Tertullian: 'What has Athens to do with Jerusalem, the Academy with the Temple?' They are calling for an unwavering adherence to the Anglican formularies, and also for a rejection of Lambeth's dithering and failure to enforce discipline upon those who have spurned the faith.

1.2.2. *Catholic*

Secondly, Anglican orthodoxy is *catholic,* in the sense that it is universal, applicable to all mankind. It can be no other if it is to be faithful to our Lord Jesus' prayer, 'that they all may be one, Father, just as You are in me and I am in You' (John 17:21). It must also be guided by St Paul's vision of the church as 'one body and one Spirit – just as you were called to one hope when you were called – one Lord, one faith, one baptism, one God and Father of all, who is over all and through all and in all' (Ephesians 4:4-6).

Anglican orthodoxy is catholic in that it values the catholic creeds and the ecumenical Councils of the early Church, recognizing that these have provided a 'rule of faith' that is derived from Scripture. While honouring the creeds, Anglican orthodoxy also upholds the substance of the Protestant confessions, recognizing that they contain key insights into the truth of the Gospel. In particular, it offers the Articles of Religion as an abiding contribution to the wider Christian church, and claims them as normative for its members.

Anglican orthodoxy agrees with the historic traditions

that 'praying shapes believing', and that liturgies are of great importance, both in communicating the faith and in sustaining Christian disciples. In particular, it sees the classic Book of Common Prayer (1662), and its authentic translations and modernizations, as expressing the substance of the faith in the context of worship. As with the Articles, it sees the Prayer Book as constituting a lasting contribution to the wider Christian church. Anglican orthodoxy incorporates a variety of ceremonials and styles of worship. It upholds the importance of the sacraments of baptism and Holy Communion as 'effectual signs of grace'. And it values the office and role of bishops in maintaining the faith across space and time.

In response to Christ's Great Commission, the scope of Anglican orthodoxy is worldwide, embracing 'every nation, tribe, people and language' (Revelation 7:9). By God's providence, the Anglican Communion is represented in every region of the world, by Christians from the different races, ethnic groups and cultures which emerged from the heritage of the British empire, who now belong to indigenous and autonomous churches. Anglican orthodoxy is also ecumenical in spirit. It is eager to participate in ecumenical dialogues and partnerships, with Roman Catholics and the Orthodox, and with various Protestant bodies, e.g., through the Lausanne movement.

It is this very desire, to maintain the true unity of the Body, that has led many orthodox Anglicans to unite together, in the face of the false Christianity that has sprung up within the Communion. The current crisis for Anglican orthodoxy is, in fact, part of a wider crisis among the historic churches of the West. As J.I. Packer puts it:

> Time was when Western Christendom's deepest division was between relatively homogeneous Protestant churches and a relatively homogeneous Church of Rome. Today,

however, the deepest and most hurtful division is between theological conservatives ("conservationists" I would rather call them), who honor the Christ of the Bible and the historic creeds and confessions, and theological liberals and radicals who for whatever reason do not; and this division splits the older Protestant bodies and the Roman Catholic communion equally, from the inside.

(*Evangelicals and Catholics Together*, pp.171-172)

The determination of some Provinces to break fellowship with theological liberals and radicals is not a sign of divisiveness, but of their commitment to genuine catholicity, in the same way that Athanasius kept separate from the Arians for the sake of the unity of truth.

1.2.3.   *Charismatic*

'You will receive power when the Holy Spirit has come upon you' (Acts 1:8). The Christian church from its very beginning is a charismatic church, waiting on God the Holy Spirit and ministering His gifts.   While Anglicans have at times dismissed the manifestations of the Spirit as 'enthusiasm', and excluded movements like Methodism which sought to promote spiritual holiness, true Anglican orthodoxy recognizes that the presence and power of the Holy Spirit are essential to its life and mission.

The Spirit is the engine of mission, sending out Gospel witnesses to the ends of the earth. Anglicanism has had a mixed record in this regard. Much of the most effective mission work overseas was accomplished on the fringes of the Church of England, through voluntary societies. Nevertheless, the gospel did go out through hundreds of committed Anglican missionaries, many of whom paid the ultimate price for their calling. These missionaries laid a foundation that has been built on by the indigenous leaders of the Global South Churches.   Now these Churches are themselves evangelizing the peoples within and across their national borders.

Anglicans have also been influenced by the spiritual revivals of the twentieth century. In East Africa, two types of spiritual dynamism emerged, the East African revival, flowing out of Rwanda in 1935, and the more recent Pentecostal and charismatic movements. The former movement emphasized the power of Christ's sacrificial death in relation to the believer; the latter emphasized the revitalizing of congregational worship and praise. Both of these have Western roots, but they have been indigenized and expressed in categories of traditional religion, including glossolalia, exorcism and prophecy.

1.3.   Anglican orthodox discipline

Anglican orthodoxy was originally part of an 'Erastian' vision of a national church, established in English law. The first Lambeth Conference recognized that governance of the new Churches of the empire was best achieved through a commitment to uniform faith and order, with discipline among the members being executed by national synods. Affirming this view, the bishops at Lambeth 1930 argued that in the extreme case of a member Church diverging from this faith and order, 'formal action would belong to the several Churches of the Anglican Communion individually', with advice from the Lambeth Conference.

Roger Beckwith has noted (*Churchman* 2003, pp.359-361) that this system of governance resembles the way in which autonomous Eastern Orthodox Churches exercise discipline, by excommunicating errant member Churches. Beckwith argues that, in the current situation, with the so-called Instruments of Unity unwilling or unable to enforce Communion discipline in the matter of homosexuality,

Anglican bishops and synods in the Global South have, perhaps unwittingly, adopted the Orthodox mode of inter-Church discipline.

This is not to say that orthodox Anglican Churches intend to splinter, with each 'doing what is right in his own eyes'. In 2002, they proposed a careful process of communal discipline, called 'To Mend the Net', only to see it disappear in the gears of the Communion bureaucracy. Again, the Global South Primates accepted the Archbishop of Canterbury's appeal, in 2003, to defer the disciplining of TEC for a year, only to have the 'Windsor process' drag on to Lambeth 2008 and beyond. Some continue to hope that an Anglican Covenant will result in a clear statement of orthodoxy, which will require the heterodox to conform or else walk apart. Others have concluded that the Covenant itself will be diluted and delayed, and that it is necessary, therefore, to come together with a renewed common vision of Anglican orthodoxy, free from the present distractions and machinations.

The central affirmation of Scripture, and of our Anglican Creeds, is that Jesus is Lord. What does this imply for our life and work? To this we turn.

2. The Lordship of Christ, in the Church and in mission

'Jesus is Lord' (I Corinthians 12:3): this confession, which is only spoken as the result of the Holy Spirit's work in the heart of a believer, is fundamental to Christianity. The truth that Jesus is Lord also underpins and connects these two topics: the Lordship of Christ in the Church, and the Lordship of Christ in mission.

2.1. The Lordship of Christ in the Church

2.1.1. The Lordship of Christ and the Trinity

The truth that Jesus is Lord must itself be seen in the light of orthodox Christian belief: we believe in one living and true God, of one Substance and in three Persons, Father, Son and Holy Spirit, who exist in mutual indwelling love.

Indeed, the Bible tells us that in this indwelling network of love, the Father loves the Son. This is expressed by the voice from heaven at Jesus' baptism and also his transfiguration (Matthew 3:17 and 17:5) and asserted by Jesus himself (John 5:20). The Father shows his paternal generosity in at least three respects: first, providing the Son with a people; secondly, giving the Son, after his resurrection and ascension, Lordship over all things for all time, and thirdly, giving the Son authority to exercise judgment at his Second Coming. We shall investigate these gifts of the Father to the Son in turn.

Before we do so, we glory in the fact that this does not exhaust the account of love between the Persons of the Trinity. While the Father's love is shown in paternal generosity, Jesus the Son loves the Father; in the Incarnation

Jesus' obedience is grounded in his love for his Father (John 14:31). The Son loves as a son should, obeying his Father. Indeed, it is out of this love for his Father that Jesus the Son submits to being sent by his Father into the world (John 3:16), and takes human nature – as the Nicene Creed and Chalcedonian Definition express it – for us and for our salvation.

This eternal relationship of mutual love is reflected in the graciousness with which the triune God creates the cosmos from nothing, with blessing (Genesis 1:28, 2:3). It is also reflected in God's merciful act of saving sinful and enslaved human creatures, blessing them with the forgiveness of sins and also adoption (Ephesians 1:3-14).

2.1.2. *The Father gives the Son a people (Colossians 1:13,14): Jesus the Deliverer*[4]

St Paul writes:

> He [the Father] has rescued us from the power of darkness and transferred us into the kingdom of his beloved Son, in whom we have redemption, the forgiveness of sins. (Colossians 1:13,14) (NRSV)

This speaks of the time before we became Christians, a time when we were not free, but under an alien dominion, in fact an alien dominion characterized by darkness and death.

We can speak of this from an African and South American perspective, and also a Western one. In African and South American contexts the truth of Colossians 1:13f is evident in the struggle to rid men and women of the

---

4   See Michael Fape, *Powers in Encounter with Power*, chapter 7 (Fearn, Ross-shire: Christian Focus Publications, 2003).

entanglement and entrapment of the powers of darkness.[5] Those under the oppressive rule of demonic powers mainly turn to the gospel message in great distress, looking to find release and sure relief. This will bring in a reign of peace and the assurance of a more fulfilled life. But by demonstrating who Christ is for us today, within the African and South American contexts, we see God in action, subduing demonic forces that regularly put up a strong fight to keep their victims in perpetual custody.

The result that the preaching of the gospel produces among unbelievers, after their conversion, shows clearly that the Christian faith indeed gives the reality of true redemption. The rescue operation that Christ carried out for those previously in bondage to demonic powers, clearly demonstrates that Christ has indeed come to preach deliverance to those in bondage, and freedom to those being oppressed by the kingdom of darkness. Being in Christ now, there is no longer anything to fear. Believers experience the reality of Hebrews 2:14-15 and the victory of Christ that these verses describe. When unbelievers are completely set free by

---

5   Principalities and powers are real phenomena in the world, as African and South American theologians and believers recognize (see Michael Fape *op cit.* and *Contra la Sagrada Resignación* by Alfredo Neufeld El Lector, 2006). These may mean nothing to Westerners, but not so with other Christians. For instance, in the words of Peter O'Brien, 'Any study of the principalities and powers quickly runs into problems of language, for the apostle Paul (not to mention other New Testament writers) uses terminology that is strange to us ... The problem lies with many contemporary Western theologians and their cultural conditioning; they have allowed the latter to dictate their understanding of the biblical texts with the result that an increasingly fashionable view, viz., that the Pauline powers designate modern socio-political structures, has become the new orthodoxy'. (P. T. O'Brien, 'Principalities and Powers: Opponents of the Church' in *Biblical Interpretation and the Church: Text and Context*, edited by D. A. Carson, (Exeter: The Paternoster Press, 1984), p.129, and D. A. Carson, *The Gagging of God* (Michigan: Zondervan, 2002).)

the power of God, as Warneck has rightly noted:

> They no longer need to give up their cattle for sacrifices and festival; they are no longer compelled to involve themselves in debt to meet the demands of the priest; they are no longer afraid of the magicians and magic.[6]

Westerners will usually be far less conscious of the reality of spiritual warfare impinging on their daily lives. There is, in any event, a deep-rooted anti-supernaturalism in much Western thought (including an incredulity about Biblical miracles), and Western ideals of autonomy resist the thought of being under any dominion. Yet the testimony of the Bible is that one may indeed be a child of Satan, in the Johannine sense of doing Satan's will (John 8:44), without consciously owning the fact but rather denying it (John 8:41, 48). And, in truth, Westerners certainly know the reality of not being able to do the good they should, and also of bondage to the wealth they have created: 'spirits oppressed by pleasure, wealth and care.'[7]

Yet the Father has transferred us to the kingdom of His Son, whom He loves. It is a kingdom of light and life. And this deliverance is to the kingdom of the one who redeems us. Redemption, in verse 14, is explained as the forgiveness of sins. This alerts us to two points.

First, our place under the alien dominion of darkness is no innocent victimhood. Victims and oppression certainly exist in the world, but a victim culture exists too, and its

---

6   John Warneck, *The Living Forces of the Gospel: Experiences of a Missionary in Animistic Heathendom* (London: Oliphant, Anderson & Ferrier, 1909), p.234.

7   From Timothy Dudley-Smith's hymn, 'Lord, for the years your love has kept and guided'.

unhealthy nature has been well-documented.[8] The risk, for the person who portrays himself simply in the role of victim, is that he feels justified in manipulating others, including God, while distorting the truth about his own fallenness. By contrast, an accurate account of human subjection to alien dominion must include mention of our own sin. A purely therapeutic view of the human problem is false, because it underplays the wonders of Jesus' actions for us: he saved us by his sacrificial, propitiatory death *while we were yet sinners* (Romans 5:8).

Secondly, our existence is now in another kingdom. Salvation does not mean complete autonomy, for salvation is incorporation into the community of the kingdom of the Son. But our king is the one who has died for us, and we are no longer under a dominion that brings us death. Yet this kingdom has kingly features, which has implications for its members. As members of the Son's kingdom, we are to show obedience and loyalty, for the Son is King, and as loyal subjects we look to the words he himself has spoken, or caused others of his servants to speak.

In this kingdom we are in unity with Christ and, because we are each in him, we are consequently in unity with each other (Ephesians 4:5). In this way our salvation is a salvation into a people, the new humanity who are in Christ and no longer in Adam. Being in the kingdom of Jesus is

---

8   S. Karpman describes the Victim Triangle in his influential article, 'Fairy Tales and Script Drama Analysis', *Transactional Analysis Bulletin* (1968), vol. 7, no.26, pp.39-43. Christopher Lasch, in *The Culture of Narcissism* (New York: W.W. Norton, 1979), develops aspects of victim culture. For consideration of some basic theological issues surrounding manipulation in a victim culture, see M. J. Ovey, 'Victim chic? The rhetoric of victimhood', *Cambridge Papers* (2006), no.15, part I.

what marks us out as the people of God, the Church. Other major Biblical motifs concerning the Church also stress the supremacy of Jesus Christ among his people: the Church is a temple whose chief cornerstone is Jesus; the Church is the bride of Christ, and the Church is the body of which Jesus is the head.

Our transfer from the kingdom of darkness to the kingdom of the Son is associated with the gracious, kindly work of the Holy Spirit, giving us hearts of flesh in place of hearts of stone. In this work God is pleased to use the instrument of His Word written, which is a Word both inspired by the Spirit, and applied by him to our hearts.

The Spirit is Himself linked with the gifts that the ascended and reigning Jesus gives to the Church. He confirms our identity as children of God and heirs (Galatians 4:6f), and himself intercedes for us (Romans 8:27) as well as endowing the people of God as he sees fit for their tasks of service in the kingdom of the Son.

2.1.3. *The Father gives the Son Lordship over all*

St Matthew records:

> And Jesus came and said to them, 'All authority in heaven and on earth has been given to me. Go therefore and make disciples of all nations, baptizing them in the name of the Father and of the Son and of the Holy Spirit, and teaching them to obey everything that I have commanded you. And remember, I am with you always, to the end of the age. (Matthew 28:18-20) (NRSV)

The gift to the Son of 'all authority' means that there are enormous implications for the subjects of his kingdom.

First, Jesus' people have both a mandate and a responsibility to evangelise. They need no permission from any other authority, since all other authorities are themselves subject to the Lordship of Jesus, not independent of him, and certainly not higher than him. This matters a great deal at a time when states and cultures seek to restrain the message of the Gospel, either by outright bans on Christian evangelism or by censoring some parts of Biblical teaching. The scope of this mandate to evangelise is 'all nations': the good news of Christ's Lordship and salvation is not to be restricted by arbitrary human choice based on race, class, wealth, perceived importance, prestige, ability or potential.

Moreover, everyone who has received the gift of salvation, and been set free from the kingdom of darkness, is also commanded to be a faithful herald of the good news. This is a question of obedience.

We will briefly review the context in which this heralding of faith takes place. God's redemptive love reached its apex in Christ's death on the Cross. But this is inseparable from the resurrection which authenticates Christ's victory over the power of death and sin. However, Christ promised that on his return to his Father the Holy Spirit would come, from the Father and the Son, as Comforter. And so Jesus' ascension inaugurates the ministry of the Holy Spirit, who continues the work of conviction, conversion and sanctification of believers, making them ready for the second coming of Christ. The Holy Spirit works remarkably in the *new man*, instilling in him a sense of urgency to pursue the task of evangelism, in obedience to the Great Commission, and promising that those who believe will be followed by 'signs' (Acts 2:19). And Christ, in the power of the Holy Spirit, has promised to be with his people to the end of the age (Matthew 28:20).

Secondly, Christ's people are constrained in what they say. They are commanded to teach people to obey '*everything that I [Jesus] have commanded you*'. And so we are to preach what Christ has mandated, *his* Word rather than ours, and not, in our independent wisdom, more or less. Christ's people are properly seen as stewards of the apostolic faith that has been handed down. They have neither the authority nor the wisdom to re-write the words of Christ, in ways that may be more palatable to a disbelieving and sinful human heart. Such a move tragically robs the Gospel of saving power, and means that those addressed in this way remain in the dominion of darkness. This duty to teach all that Christ commands goes beyond the simple proclamation of the Gospel, for we are to make *disciples*. Hence the importance of, for example, the catechizing of new believers.[9]

Thirdly, in this obedience that Matthew 28:18 calls for, there can be no competing loyalty. This follows from the scope and the timing of the gift of authority to Jesus. The ascended Christ reigns *now* in this present age, despite its continuing rebellion, and over all. Thus competing authorities are even *now,* in reality, subject to Christ. No aspect of human life can claim to be independent of the reign of Christ: all, whether political, economic or artistic, is under Him.[10] We therefore do not conform ourselves to this present age (compare Romans 12:2), for we are a pilgrim people, living in the present world, which we know is passing away, and looking beyond it to its true lord. We are prepared, if necessary, to give our lives now in anticipation of the world to come, which is the real world.

Fourthly, while the content of what Christ has entrusted to us is not ours to alter, modify, deny or add to, effective teaching presupposes effective communication within particular contexts. Authentic obedience to the Great

---

9   As with the Church of Nigeria's *Operation 1-1-3*.
10   Compare Abraham Kuyper's view that as Christ is lord of all creation, each 'sphere' of human activity in creation is properly subject to Jesus.

Commission of Matthew 28 thus has a dynamic aspect, seeking apt ways to communicate in new historical and local situations, while safeguarding the deposit of faith itself. For, as a pilgrim people, we relate to, but are not conformed to, the present age.

Fifthly, Matthew 28:18-20 must also be seen in conjunction with the Lucan commission (Luke 24:47-48). The communication of the truth of Christ's kingship and his commands is not mere information, a piece of intellectual news to the effect that authority is now vested in Christ. Rather, it is a message containing a summons to repentance and also the offer of forgiveness. It presupposes a human race which, after Genesis 3, is predisposed against God, and whose rebellion and disbelief merit punishment and require forgiveness. The message of the Cross is that Christ has purchased this forgiveness: he saves us from the wrath to come (1 Thessalonians 1:9,10).

2.1.4. *The Father gives the Son authority to judge (John 5:22)*

There is another, future, dimension to the Lordship that the Father gives to the Son. God in his goodness will one day set the world to rights, and this involves the execution of justice. God has given Jesus the prerogative to be the Judge of all at the end of the age. It is true that he came at first to be the 'Lamb of God who takes away the sin of the world' (John 1:29), but then he comes the second time to be the Judge of all, because the Father has given him all authority to judge men and women, for heaven or hell. Repentance is therefore commanded to all, so as to avoid Jesus condemning us as our Judge at his second coming (Acts 17:30). This is a day for which God's people are hoping, because Jesus comes to reign eternally in glory and justice at his second coming, and also because God in his mercy promises forgiveness to those who turn to God in repentance and faith. God's people are called on to wait in hope for that day (1 Thessalonians 1:10), to be on watch for it, and meanwhile to proclaim to others God's promise of mercy and to do works that befit those who 'belong to the day' (1 Thessalonians 5:8). We will consider, shortly, the deeds 'of the day' and the mission of the Church under the Lordship of Christ.

2.1.5. *Summary*

We have now seen the Lordship of Christ in the Church in three different dimensions. First, the Church is the kingdom of the Son, and God has transferred men, women and children into this kingdom, not into complete autonomy, or a spiritual republic. There are no people of God except in the kingdom of the Son. Secondly, Jesus the Son currently has all authority and, ascended, reigns now over the cosmos. His people recognize his authority on earth now; they do not simply look forward to the future reign of Christ. Thirdly, Jesus' people do look to the future consummation of this existing reality, when Jesus the Son will return to judge the world and finally deliver his people.

2.2. The Lordship of Christ in mission

2.2.1. *Meeting the world*

The world we meet is created by God and upheld by him in his providence and love. The signs of his continuing common grace bear witness to this. Yet the world is marred, diverse and complex. However, we meet this world in the light of the Lordship of Christ, and since a servant is not greater than his or her master, our encounter with the world must replicate the features of Jesus' encounter.

Our encounter with the world, over which Jesus is Lord, is marked by the knowledge that we and others are created by the triune God and, uniquely, created in his image.

In our relationships with others, we realize that we are dealing with people who belong to God (Psalm 24:1,2), created by him for his purposes in creation. It is for this reason that we have a duty to treat others with respect, dignity and love (see Proverbs 14:31).

We know, too, that humanity has marred itself by sin, and enslaved itself, and that in this slavery humans treat each other not as creatures made in the image of God but as things, to be owned, used and exploited. We recognize, therefore, that the human world is one marked by victimization, as well as being marked by guilt before God.

We know, next, that there is an exclusivity to Christ's Lordship, such that humans cannot mix allegiances (1 Corinthians 10:14ff), seeking to serve two or more 'lords' (Jesus and Apollo, Jesus and Buddha, Jesus and hedonism). We also know that to deny this Lordship is to refuse salvation, since only the Lordship of Jesus will save a person.

We know, finally, that Jesus' Lordship is not only about saving people, but also about serving them. Of course we must serve by proclaiming the Gospel, but the principle of neighbourliness (Luke 10:25-37) also requires more practical ways of help, what in a South American context would be referred to as *misión integral.* For, while he was here on earth, Jesus was concerned not only for the spiritual well-being of his audiences, but also for their physical needs, which he met with great compassion. In Matthew's account of the feeding of the five thousand (Matthew 14:13-21), it is interesting that, after preaching the good news to a multitude, Jesus commanded his *disciples* to give the people something to eat (verse 16), before providing the food himself.

2.2.2. *Other faiths*

These considerations mark the encounter of the people of God with other faiths. Remembering the truth of the words of Augustine – who also had to face a world of other faiths – that 'our heart is restless until it rests in you'[11], we can recognize that there is an authenticity to the spiritual restlessness and yearning for eternity and transcendence that many other faiths seek to meet, for we know that these things lie in the human heart. But authentic, saving, rest is only found in Jesus Christ. No one comes to the Father except through the Son (John 14:6).

Particular mention must be made of the Church's encounter with secularism. For secularism is the world-view that seeks to exclude the Lordship of Christ from this world; by denying there is any reality but the reality of this world, it denies any Lordship to Jesus. A Christian response is not to repudiate this world, for the world continues to be God's creation, containing signs of his goodness to us. Since Christians are *in* the world, though they do not belong to it, their lives should be a demonstration to the world of God's goodness and love, and the Church should offer ministries that, uniquely, bring the touch of heaven to earth. There is no question of compromising the faith in this. Our light must shine in the world, so that non-Christians see the good deeds of Christians and glorify the name of God (Matt. 5:16).

2.2.3. *A world of need*

The world we meet is also a world of pressing need, in many ways.

A primary area where the world needs the ministry of

---

11   *Confessions* I.1

the Church is that of family and sexuality: 'Faithful and fruitful mission will include the protection and promotion of sound marriages, healthy families and holy singleness.'[12] For God has given us marriage and family life as gifts in creation (Genesis 2:18ff), elements of common grace for fallen humanity. Marriage manifests the equal value of men and women before God, and also their complementarity. Marriage between man and woman is the context in which the good (for God creates all things good), yet powerful (as the *Song of Songs* notes), gift of sexuality is to be cherished, respected and enjoyed. With respect to the family, this is the most basic unit of all social organizations, and is rightly called a micro-society. Without healthy family life, the life of society can only suffer.

Just as God, in creation, establishes the true purpose for human existence, so too he establishes the purposes for his gifts; these are to be enjoyed according to his commands. Thus, Genesis 2:18ff establishes the norm of monogamous heterosexual marriage for the exercise of the gift of sexuality. As with other gifts of God, this gift may be twisted to serve purposes other than those for which it was given. Such sinful distortions may occur in different ways in different cultures and places. We see with sadness the practice of polygamy in some African contexts, and we observe, too, the Western acceptance of serial monogamy, in which marriage is followed by casual divorce and subsequent re-marriage, not once but several times. South Americans may likewise feel that the ideal of Genesis 2:18ff has not been adequately presented within their cultures. But the biblical pattern for marriage, that it should be a life-long relationship between a

---

12   Para 22, *Anglican Life in Mission*, Consultation Statement, EFAC International Consultation July 2003, Limuru, Kenya

man and a woman, provides the context in which we must see the current issue, within the Anglican Communion, of homosexual practice or same-sex relations being described as marriage. A statement from the Province of the Southern Cone has rightly said:

> We affirm that ... adultery, sex outside of marriage and homosexual unions are all contrary to God's purposes for our humanity. We likewise deplore homophobia, hypocrisy and sexual abuse and seek to acknowledge and overcome such sins.[13]

A Church which fails to call back to this norm (of Genesis 2:18ff) the culture to which it is sent, risks condemning both itself and the culture. It condemns itself because it is conforming to the world and not to the teaching that Jesus has commanded, and it condemns the culture, because the erosion of family life corrodes both the individual and the society of which he or she is a part.

In the area of health and social services, need will differ from one society or nation to another. In countries where people are living with HIV and AIDS, the Church must continue to be an active participant because of the love and hope that lie at the heart of the Gospel. The Church of Uganda's emphasis on behaviour change and other interventions has been rightly praised by those outside the Church. Similarly the Church of Kenya has contributed remarkably, through its empowering educational programmes. Of great significance was the Provincial Action Committee on AIDS (PACA), an initiative of the Church of Nigeria, which was inaugurated in June 2004. Through this body, the Church has been able to minister to the needs of local people in different parts of Nigeria, thereby making the

---

13   Quoted in Para 22 of *Anglican Life in Mission.*

Church relevant to people when they are hurting, as well as educating them on the need for a well-guarded sexual life. We should mention, too, the pressing need to care for malaria sufferers, in view of the huge impact of this disease; in Kenya, more children die of malaria than AIDS. Elsewhere other troubles arise, such as the increase of tuberculosis in South America.

The principles we have looked at so far must be applied also to poverty, and some of the problems associated with it. If Christ is Lord, we must remember that he is lord of the economic sphere as well as everything else. But some groups and races – for example indigenous South Americans and some Aboriginal groups in Australia – remain effectively untouched by aid programmes. Defiance of Christ's laws in this sphere is no less serious than it would be in other areas of life, and just as we would speak against adultery, whoever did it, so too we should speak against exploitation and corruption. In the economic sphere, perhaps especially, the duty of being a good neighbour, in a way that is both loving and responsible, must be recognized. Both elements matter here: there is a pressing need to love one's neighbour, true, but there are ways of providing support and showing concern that are ultimately irresponsible, even if well-intentioned. We think, for instance, of the way that support to the poverty-stricken, both within individual nations and between nations, has sometimes helped create a demeaning culture of dependency, and perpetuated problems of vulnerability and indignity rather than solving them. Neighbourliness that is genuinely loving, moreover, may well display a different attitude in matters of development, exercising patience and looking less to self-interest.

In its mission to bring complete wholeness to society, the Church needs to encourage members to gain financial independence. For this reason various Churches are trying to initiate economic empowerment programmes, which enable Christians to get involved in productive economic ventures, without being worldly in implementation.

2.3. Epilogue

We have stressed that in the Church, and in the Church's mission to the world, Jesus is Lord. Such an assertion is sometimes thought to be a denial of love, in that Lordship and love are thought to be antithetical, contradictory notions. Yet Jesus himself is emphatic that love and Lordship *do* go together, and in two respects. We know that he loves us, for he gave himself for us, and yet he insists that he is our Lord. Also, he tells us that our love is to be shown in obedience to his commands (John 14:15; 2 John 6). This means that disobedience to what Jesus commands is a denial of love, for him, for his people, for the world.

In affirming obedience to Jesus as Lord, how should we expect his authority to be exercised, discerned, expressed and obeyed? To this we turn.

3. How do we know the truth about God, and his purposes?

The current crisis within the Anglican Communion is, in very large measure, generated by conflicting views on how Christians come to know God and his purposes. Just what is it that constitutes the final authority, when it comes to our ideas about God and what he is doing in the world? What determines how we ought to live, as those he has redeemed in Christ? Are these things to be determined by what seems reasonable to the larger culture in which we operate as Anglican Christians? Are the determinations of synods and ecclesiastical councils or conferences decisive? Are we to expect direct leadings of the Spirit, which make the right course of action seem intuitive? Or has God promised to make his mind known in some other way?

In recent years some have sought to redefine the answers to these questions, in ways which are deeply contrary to authentic Anglicanism as described in the Thirty-nine Articles, the Book of Common Prayer and the Homilies. This means that a fresh statement of the real nature of authority within authentic Anglicanism is urgently needed, as is a more explicit treatment of how we ought to approach the task of reading and explaining Scripture in the light of that statement. However, it is equally important that our consideration of this subject take a form which is consistent with its own conclusions. This will mean that it must be shaped by a rigorous biblical theology.

3.1. Christ, the authority in the Church

All authority in heaven and on earth has been given to Jesus Christ.[14] As Israel's Messiah and the eternal Son of the Father, he stands over all other claims to authority, however they might be constituted. He alone is the appointed judge of all human life and activity.[15] Every decision is subject to his scrutiny. He alone is the appointed saviour of the world, the only hope of all men and women, and his is the one name given under heaven by which we must be saved.[16] His lordship is the goal for which all things were made.[17] It is the great unchanging purpose of God the Father to bring all things together under the headship of God the Son by the powerful work of God the Spirit.[18] While many ignore or defy his authority at present, the day is most surely coming when every knee will bow and every tongue confess that Jesus Christ is Lord, and this cannot help but demonstrate the glory of God the Father.[19]

More specifically, Jesus Christ is the only head of the Church.[20] He is the one who is building his Church and not even the gates of Hades can prevail against it.[21] No human consensus or claim to institutional legitimacy can be grounds to modify or set aside his rule in even the most minute measure. The Church is forever dependent on Christ. He is present as his people gather in his name, just as he

---

14   Matt. 28:18.
15   Acts 17:30–31.
16   Acts 4:12; Eph. 2:12; Jn 14:6.
17   Col. 1:16.
18   Eph. 1:10.
19   Phil. 2:10–11.
20   Eph. 5:23.
21   Matt. 16:18.

promised.[22] He poured out his Spirit on his people on the Day of Pentecost and by this same Spirit he gives gifts to his people today so that they might serve each other and grow into his likeness.[23] Believers are exhorted to let his word dwell in them richly.[24] Christian discipleship is fundamentally a recognition of Christ's lordship, his right to direct the life and thought of the redeemed people of God. There can be no Church where the authority of Christ to call us to faith and repentance – to challenge our cultural commitments, our personal preferences and our traditions – is neglected.

Christ exercises this authority in the Churches throughout these last days by his word through his Spirit. Just as during his earthly ministry Jesus' words stilled the storm, expelled the demons, healed the sick and raised the dead, so today they nourish faith and direct the lives of those who follow him.[25] Jesus leads his people today by his word addressed to them as his disciples. Likewise, the Spirit who rested upon Jesus throughout his earthly ministry attends his word today, transforming lives by that word as men and women are convicted and convinced of its truth.[26] Faith, that genuine confidence and trust in Christ's good word which gives rise to a wholehearted obedience, is the result of the Spirit's work in the human heart.[27] In this way it becomes clear that the word and the Spirit are not to be considered as two separate and potentially competing means, by which the living and active Christ operates in the Church over its long

---

22   Matt. 18:20.
23   Acts 2:32–33; Eph. 4:11–14; 1 Cor. 12:4–7.
24   Col. 3:16.
25   e.g Mk 4:35–41; 9:14–29; 1:40–45; 5:35–43.
26   Jn 16:7–15.
27   Jn 3:1–8; Eph. 2:8–9; 3:14–19; 2 Cor. 4:13–14.

history. Christ rules by his word through his Spirit.

This is seen most clearly in the Scriptures. The Old Testament is the written form of the word of God carried on the breath of God.[28] The apostolic writings share this same character, by virtue of Christ's promise and commission.[29] The Bible lies at the centre of the Church's life precisely because it is the Spirit-inspired written form of the word of God, by which Christ's authority is exercised until he returns.[30] These Scriptures are not limited in truth and relevance because they were spoken in the first century, nor are they bound by time, culture or space. Rather, they express the mind of God who knows all things as they truly are. This is why they are never dated or outmoded. They never need to be corrected in the light of new advances in knowledge. Rather, they remain eternally relevant and authoritative. Yet the Scriptures are not an alternative to the dynamic personal presence of Christ, the Church's Lord. By his word and through his Spirit he is present 'until the end of the age'.

Any other authority exercised amongst God's people must be subject to the authority of Christ, and so subject to the authority of the Scriptures. It can only ever be the authority of obedience, shaped and circumscribed by the teaching of the Bible as the written word of God. The doctrine and lifestyle of all who exercise leadership among the Churches is to be tested by the teaching of Scripture, as was the case with the apostles themselves.[31] There is no place

---

28   2 Tim. 3:16–17; 2 Pet. 1:20–21.
29   Jn 14:15–26; Matt. 28:18–20; 2 Pet. 3:15–16.
30   See the following subsection of this document for further discussion of the nature and origin of Scripture, and the consequences for both its place in the church and the way it is read by Christians.
31   Acts 17:10–11; Gal. 2.

in Christian leadership for those who are committed to patterns of behaviour on account of which 'the wrath of God is coming'.[32] Furthermore, the manner of leadership among the Churches is likewise to be tested against the example of Christ, as attested in the Scriptures. Obedience, and a determination to serve rather than to dominate, are the constituent elements of that genuine humility the Churches are to expect in all who lead according to the pattern of Christ.[33] Such leaders (no matter how exalted their title or claim to jurisdiction) do not stand over the Scriptures, determining what is acceptable today and what is not. Instead they sit under the Scriptures, prepared to be challenged and corrected themselves by the written word of God. Repentance in the light of the teaching of Scripture is to be a constant characteristic of their lives. They forfeit the authority that has been delegated to them when this is not the case. This is, tragically, much more than simply a hypothetical reality. The need to stand against false teaching and the abuse of authority within the Churches, throughout the entire period until the Lord returns, is anticipated by Jesus himself and by his apostles.[34]

A similar dynamic is at work in confessional statements, such as the Thirty-nine Articles of Religion. These are genuinely authoritative documents, but their authority is always dependent upon their faithful reflection of the teaching of Scripture as the word of the Church's only Lord. This is explicitly recognised, in the case of the Thirty-nine Articles, by Articles VI, VII and XX, while Article VIII makes the same point with reference to the ancient creeds.

---

32   Eph. 5:5–6; Col. 3:5–6.
33   Mk 10:42–45; Phil. 2:3–11.
34   Matt. 24:3–14; 1 Tim. 6:3–10; 2 Tim 3:1–5.

The interpretative grid against which the Articles are to be read is the teaching of Scripture, just as the Articles are presented as an attempt to distil that teaching on a number of important issues. The words, grammar and historical context of the Articles make clear that they have a real but contingent authority, arising as they do in a world where councils and other ecclesiastical assemblies 'may err and sometimes have erred, even in things pertaining unto God'.

While it is sometimes said that the three-legged stool of Scripture, tradition and reason is a mutually referring and informing authority for Anglicans – a concept usually but inaccurately attributed to comments by Richard Hooker in his *Of the Lawes of Ecclesiastical Polity* – the idea, in fact, finds no support in Scripture, nor in the foundational documents of Anglicanism (The Thirty-nine Articles, The Book of Common Prayer and The Homilies). Scripture stands alone, above both the tradition of the Churches and the carefully reasoned arguments of the human mind.[35] The Christian tradition is not to be despised or treated lightly, but it is always reformable on the basis of biblical teaching. And human reason is a gift of God, which remains useful even on this side of the Fall. It is actively employed in the reading of Scripture. However, it too needs reformation by the teaching of Scripture. In contrast Scripture, as the written word of God, needs no reformation or correction, either by the consensus of Christians or by the fresh insights of human reason.

On occasion, departures from biblical teaching have

---

35   This is in fact what Hooker taught: 'What Scripture doth plainly deliver, to that *the first place of credit* and obedience is due; *the next* whereunto is whatever any man can necessarily conclude by force of reason; *after these* the voice of the church succeedeth.' Hooker, *Lawes,* V.8.2.

been justified by appeal to the notion of prophecy. Those who advocate innovation in Christian thought and practice insist that their proposals are a new word from the Spirit. However, in the Old Testament and in the New, claims to possess new prophetic words are not self-authenticating; the new prophetic words are to be tested for their consistency with the teaching of the Scriptures.[36] A truly prophetic word not only 'comes to pass' in the world, it also reflects the teaching of the Bible. True prophets call people back to the words that God has already spoken, demanding faith and repentance. Precisely because 'many false prophets have gone out into the world', all proposals need to be tested by the Scriptures.[37] Testing even the words of the apostles by the teaching of the Scriptures is commended in the New Testament.[38]

3.2.   The nature of Scripture, and its use in the Church

The canonical Scriptures of the Old and New Testaments are the written word of God. At the same time they are self-evidently human texts, using human words penned by human beings in particular historical, cultural and linguistic contexts. Both of these dimensions must be affirmed with equal seriousness. Human beings moved by the Holy Spirit spoke from God, and the result was texts which are God-breathed.[39] The ultimate origin of these texts in the breath of God does not do away with the significance of the contribution made by each human author and the various contexts in which they wrote. The human authors were

---

36   Deut. 13:1–5.
37   1 Jn 4:1–6.
38   Acts 17:11.
39   2 Pet. 1:19–21; 2 Tim. 3:16–17.

consciously and creatively involved as they were moved by the Spirit. Likewise, the genuine humanity of these texts is no impediment to their communication of God's thoughts, words and personal presence. These words, 'written for our instruction' by those God himself commissioned in various ways, indelibly bear the unchangeable and unchallengeable authority of God.[40]

Jesus Christ himself treated the Old Testament Scriptures as the word of God, upholding them as authoritative Scripture which ends all speculation about the nature, character and purposes of God. His appeal to the Old Testament during the temptation in the wilderness demonstrates his assessment that these words were the appropriate and final answer to the challenges posed by the ancient enemy, in stark contrast to the way the first man and woman responded to a similar challenge.[41] He regularly made a similar appeal to the words of the Old Testament in his debates with the religious leaders of his day. They ought to have read and heeded the 'word of God' – an expression he saw no need to qualify when used of an Old Testament text – and he considered it scandalous that they should set this word aside in the interests of human tradition.[42]

Jesus consistently characterised the Old Testament Scriptures as the authoritative testimony to his person and mission. They all point to him, they are fulfilled in him, and they provide the proper categories for understanding what he came to do.[43] While Jesus' own use of the Old Testament assumes a basic unity for its various texts, which is properly

---

40   Rom. 15:4.
41   Matt. 4:1–11; cf. Gen. 3:1–7.
42   Matt. 15:1–9.
43   Jn 5:39; Lk 4:16–21; Mk 10:45; Lk 22:1–23.

traced to their common origin in the breath of God, he explicitly identifies this additional unity of reference: a common testimony to God's unfolding purpose, which has now come to its climax in his own life, work and words.

It is the commission of Jesus which generates the New Testament Scriptures. He gave a particular authority to his apostles to bear witness to him, just as over the centuries the writings of the prophets had borne witness to him.[44] He promised them the Holy Spirit, who would remind them of all he had told them while he was amongst them.[45] The testimony which the Spirit would enable them to bear to Jesus was to extend 'to the end of the earth' and 'until the end of the age'.[46] The apostolic writings flow out of that commission. They are part of the discharge of the apostles' responsibility to proclaim Christ and his gospel 'to the Jew first and also to the Greek'.[47] As such they bear the authority of the Lord who commissioned the apostles and are rightly considered amongst 'the other Scriptures'.[48] Later discussion of the New Testament canon would make much of the apostolic provenance of these particular books and letters. Far from investing the New Testament with authority, the decisions of the Churches in the first few centuries acknowledged an authority which was prior to all ecclesiastical deliberation. The New Testament is Christian Scripture alongside the Old Testament, not first and foremost because the Churches received it as such, but because here is the apostolic testimony to Christ and the shape of life lived as his disciples. The Scriptures are not the product of the

---

44   Lk 24:44–48; Jn 15: 27; Acts 1:8.
45   Jn 14:25–26.
46   Acts 1:8; Matt. 28:18–20.
47   Rom. 1:14–17.
48   2 Pet. 3:15–16.

churches. Rather, Christ continues to address the Churches by these words.

As an expression of this discipleship, all Christians and authentic Christian Churches should delight in reflecting the attitude of their Lord to the Scriptures. The reading and exposition of the Scriptures is a prominent feature of our gatherings, precisely because these are the words Jesus taught us to embrace as the gift of our loving Father, given to nourish the faith of his people. God's own nature and character provide the guarantee of their goodness and effectiveness. The authority, unity, clarity and sufficiency of the Scriptures arise directly from the sovereignty and benevolence of the holy God whose written word they are.

For this reason, a faithful reading of Scripture cannot approach the biblical text with suspicion or with the intention of exposing error, contradiction or irrelevance. Such attitudes toward Scripture amount to an assault upon the character of the God who has given us this good word. The Christian assumption is always that our problems with the teaching of Scripture are our problems, rather than problems with the Bible. We have all been profoundly influenced by the Fall, in our reasoning as in every other area of our lives. Cultural bias, a sense of historical superiority, and the intellectual expressions of a deep-seated human rebellion against the rule of God through his word, can combine with our ignorance of the whole of Scripture – and our lack of attention to what is actually said in the parts we do know – to produce sophisticated manipulations of the text in our own interests, or else a self-satisfied agnosticism. It is possible actually to evade the teaching of Scripture while giving others the impression that you are taking it very seriously, 'having the appearance of godliness but denying its power'.[49]

It is only by careful attention to, and reflection upon, the Scriptures that we are able to 'test everything [and] hold fast what is good'.[50] As with every other aspect of the Christian life, in both its individual and its corporate dimensions, this faithful, attentive reflection can only be done in prayerful dependence upon the Holy Spirit. The same Spirit who was critically involved in the production of the Biblical text enables us to adopt the appropriate stance as we read it. By his enabling, Christians are to read the Scriptures as disciples eager to learn, concerned to have our thinking and behaviour corrected, so that our lives might conform more truly to the ultimate reality of God's character and purposes. In short, Christians sit humbly under the Spirit-inspired Scriptures, desiring to live holy lives as Christ's disciples.

This careful attention to the Bible involves being directed by its purpose. Mistakes can and have been made when the Bible has been read either as a scientific text, concerned to expound principles of cosmology, geology, biology and the like, or as a narrative which provides an imaginative world, against which background we come to our own conclusions about what is valuable in human life and relationships. Instead, the purposes for which Scripture was given are explicit within Scripture itself. These include: to testify to Jesus Christ with the purpose of eliciting faith and repentance; to make those who read them 'wise for salvation through faith in Christ Jesus'; to instruct us so that 'through endurance and through the encouragement of the Scriptures we might have hope'; and to teach, reprove, correct and train

---

49   2 Tim. 3:5.
50   1 Thess. 5:21.

in righteousness so that Christ's disciples might be 'competent, equipped for every good work'.[51]

Likewise, mistakes can be made when the Bible is read idiosyncratically or individualistically, with little or no regard for the communion of saints which provides the proper context for a faithful approach to Scripture. Traditional readings of Scripture may need to be challenged, because they involve a mis-step at the point of understanding the words, their context or their purpose. Conventional readings are not proper readings simply because they are conventional. However, novelty has no special privileges either. The traditional interpretation of a text must not be lightly challenged or flippantly overthrown. None of us is the first to read the Scriptures with care, humility and faith. Special care needs to be taken when a proposed new reading results in an endorsement of the culture in which we live. It is all too easy to echo the world's commitments, rather than challenge them.

A critical element of the faithful reading of Scripture is a due regard for its unity and coherence. The practice of comparing Scripture with Scripture guards against fragmentary readings which frequently misuse individual texts. Biblical theology – the study of the unfolding nature of God's revelation in salvation history, which highlights the relationship of each part of the Bible to its centre in the person, words and work of Jesus Christ – is immensely valuable in this regard. It expresses the conviction that Scripture is its own interpreter, that one of the most important resources God has given us to understand any part of the Bible is the whole Bible. Faithful Christian doctrine and ethics rely upon both an explicit appeal to biblical texts,

---

51 Jn 5:39; 20:30–31; 2 Tim. 3:14–15; Rom. 15:4; 1 Cor. 10:11; 2 Tim. 3:16–17.

and an understanding of how those texts fit within the message of the Bible as a whole. This is also the commitment which lies behind the statement in Article XX of the Thirty-nine Articles of Religion: 'And yet it is not lawful for the Church to ordain any thing that is contrary to God's Word written, neither may it so expound one place of Scripture, that it be repugnant to another'.

The word of God is given to the people of God. It is not the private possession of either a scholarly elite or any ecclesiastical hierarchy. The New Testament insistence upon the public reading of Scripture[52] assumes that the plain meaning of Scripture is accessible to all, and that it nourishes the faith of believers regardless of cultural differences or educational background. God is actively involved as we read Scripture today, transforming lives in the present as in the past through the powerful words which he has spoken, and which he caused to be written for the benefit of his people. The principal requirement is that we should be those who 'hear the word of God and keep it'.[53]

There is still a valuable place for the work of Biblical and theological scholarship. It should not be dismissed as irrelevant, particularly when it encourages a careful reading of the text we have been given, and alerts us to features we might otherwise have missed. However, care must be taken not to position Biblical scholarship as a new *magisterium*, an authoritative interpretation that is necessary if anyone is to understand the Bible. God addresses his people directly in the words of Scripture, conveyed to their hearts by his Spirit. He is able to convey clearly and effectively his message of salvation through the death and resurrection of Jesus Christ,

---

52   1 Thess. 5:27;,1 Tim. 4:13.
53   Lk. 11:28.

together with his call to faith and holy living in the light of what Jesus has done.

In the light of our affirmations of the Lordship and the authority of Jesus Christ as the Son of God, how are we to worship God the Father through him, in the power of the Spirit and in truth? To this we turn.

4. Engaging with the Anglican liturgical heritage in shaping the future

Let us all enter into the joy of the Lord![54]

4.1. Introduction to Anglican worship

Anglican worship goes back to the Reformation and, through the Reformation, to the early Church and the Bible. The Book of Common Prayer, which Archbishop Cranmer devised at the time of the Reformation, was not a new thing, but it was new in many ways. It introduced worship in the vernacular, for instance, but it inherited from the past many edifying elements of worship, and took the Bible as the norm by which to judge what to maintain and what to discard. One result of this is to be found in the exhortation at the beginning of Morning and Evening Prayer, which sets out what the service is intended to contain: thanksgiving, praise, the reading of Scripture and prayer, all in the context of repentance and forgiveness.

4.1.1. *We are a liturgical people*

Anglican worship is designedly liturgical in order to restrain the church from going astray in the way it approaches God. Anglican worship is also corporate in its intention, as the title 'Book of *Common* Prayer' implies, and it is normally led by the ordained ministry, but Christians are fully expected and encouraged to worship in private as well as in public. In

---

54   *A Paschal Sermon* by St John Chrysostom (347-407)

order to prepare people for corporate worship, the first of the long exhortations before Holy Communion in the Prayer Book reminds them about what they are doing: they have come together to receive 'the Sacrament of the Body and Blood of Christ', which they will do 'in remembrance of his meritorious Cross and Passion; whereby alone we obtain remission of our sins, and are made partakers of the kingdom of heaven.' It goes on to stress the great importance of confessing their sins and obtaining God's forgiveness before receiving the blessed Sacrament, for 'it is requisite, that no man should come to the holy Communion, but with a full trust in God's mercy, and with a quiet conscience'.

4.1.2. *We have a ministry of Word and Sacrament*

The Anglican ministry is a ministry of both word and sacraments, and both elements have a very prominent place in Prayer Book worship. The word enacted in sacrament is also a way in which people experience Christ. Article 19 of the Thirty-nine Articles lays down that one of the marks of the visible Church is that the sacraments are rightly administered. This makes the Eucharist central to the liturgical life of the Church. It is important to recognize that the heritage of the Prayer Book faith and formularies has left us with a rich and full doctrine of the Eucharist, with a strong sense of the presence of Christ, or 'real participation' to use the language of Hooker, and understanding of the nature of his sacrifice.

4.1.3. *We uphold the Creeds and our historic formularies, believing in 'one holy, catholic and apostolic Church'*

Anglican liturgy upholds its inheritance of the faith 'uniquely revealed' in the Scriptures which contain all things necessary for salvation. This faith is 'set forth' in the Creeds received by the whole Church and recited in our liturgy. These three historic Creeds, being proved 'by most certain warrants of holy Scripture', were thus retained in the Prayer Book and they are reaffirmed in the Thirty-nine Articles (Article 8) before these go on to speak of the other Biblical truths which were highlighted at the Reformation.

Anglicans uphold the teaching of the Councils of the early undivided Church, and the ecumenical norms of church order set out in the Lambeth Quadrilateral. It is timely to recall, given the great contribution of Africans in Alexandria and elsewhere to the early Church, that Anglicans have characteristically appealed to the consensus of antiquity and the voice of the Patristic Church, in support of scriptural interpretation. Affirming together our shared assent to the fundamental articles of faith is what provides the necessary and sufficient conditions for Communion. To break from affirming the common faith and mind of the Church is to fall short of these conditions for Communion and to step away from the fullness of true Christian fellowship.

The 1930 Lambeth Conference, in setting out the ideals for which the Anglican Church has always stood, stressed features that were not held to be unique to Anglicanism but rather to be 'the ideals of the Church of Christ' including 'an open Bible, a pastoral priesthood, a common worship', and 'a standard of conduct consistent with that worship and a fearless love of truth'.

Anglicans, through their commitment to membership of the *holy*, catholic and apostolic Church, are committed to upholding that holiness of life and morals which Holy Scripture sets forth and requires. Our liturgy daily reminds us of this call to holiness and amendment of life. Doctrine and morals thus come together continually in the worship of the Church; they do not stand apart from each other. 'Let your light so shine before men, that they may see your good works, and glorify your Father which is in heaven' (Matthew

5:16).

4.1.4. *We follow a liturgical calendar, a lectionary and a Catechism*

Anglicans retain a calendar of the Christian year as a means of recalling the life of our Lord and Saviour, and as a means of setting out the great truths of the Gospel in turn each year. The calendar gives a pattern to Christian worship throughout the year. Archbishop Cranmer passed on to the Anglican Church an historic lectionary with roots in the early church. The Sunday reading of Scripture was intended to ensure an orderly and doctrinally-based reading of Scripture, and the daily lectionary was designed to ensure that as much as possible of the Bible was read to congregations in their own language, every year. These aims should continue to inform such new lectionaries as Anglicans develop.

An important element in the Prayer Book was the Catechism, designed to teach the basic elements of Christian faith and worship to candidates for confirmation. A fuller Catechism was later provided, to give additional instruction. Further Catechisms may well be developed today, in continuity with this historic and Biblical faith, as an aid in mission, and as a way of enhancing the effective teaching of the faith and encouraging its ever wider propagation.

4.1.5. *We worship the Lord in spirit and in truth*

Anglican worship, with its unifying Prayer Book tradition and Biblical emphasis, has clearly upheld the benefits and dignity of the 'said prayers' and liturgy, yet we also recognize that freedom of worship that is truly in the Spirit is also an essential element of Christian life and devotion. This element has sometimes been neglected in our tradition, and we therefore welcome the openness of approved contemporary liturgies to times for spontaneous prayer, prophecy, discernment of spirits, and testimony, within the framework of ordered liturgical worship. We recognize too the need for prayerful discernment in the light of our heritage of faith and practice, and subject to Biblical norms. We believe that the Church, in the power of the Spirit, will manifest his gifts decently and in order, and with power and reverence.

4.2.   The challenges of the present

O come, let us sing unto the Lord: let us heartily rejoice in the strength of our salvation. (Psalm 95, the *Venite*)

Worship is rooted in our faith in God's work of creation, incarnation and redemption, and we seek to enter more deeply into God's life and love as those who are called to be 'partakers of the divine nature' (2 Peter 1.4). 'The visible Church of Christ is a congregation of faithful men,' states Article 19, 'in the which the pure Word of God is preached, and the Sacraments be duly administered according to Christ's ordinance'. Thus are we called, as Anglicans, to an ever deeper understanding of our heritage of structured and orderly corporate worship and private prayer, together with constant proclamation of God's Word. It is in this work as God's people – which is his body, the Church – that our identity is both formed and expressed.

We invoke the Holy Spirit as we seek to be open to God's future, and to orient ourselves ever more fully to the fulfillment of God's will. We are bound together by the bonds of shared faith and common heritage, as we seek to be one in the Lord. Our worship and liturgy, which we have received, carry the historic faith of the Church forward into the future, and in this way they challenge us to be true to our history, as evangelical, catholic and reformed. In particular, the great gift of the Book of Common Prayer is one that we continue to value, for it has done so much to define and shape the liturgy, faith and witness of our Church. This is the heritage we must deepen and renew.

4.2.1. *Daily prayer*

We are enjoined 'to pray without ceasing', and the regular daily cycle of psalms and prayer, the reading of God's Word and the singing of his praises, allows us to stand with Christ in unity with the Church of the ages. How can this heritage of morning and evening prayer be deepened and revived? How can the use of the Canticles and the recitation (musical chant) of the psalms best be renewed?

4.2.2. *The Eucharist*

The Eucharist, instituted by Christ himself, stands alone as the one great liturgical act which transcends all of time, bringing us into the great mystery which is Christ's once-for-all act of salvation. Holy Communion, as the central liturgical act of the Church, must receive due emphasis in our worship, without it excluding other important daily elements such as those of Morning and Evening Prayer.

4.2.3. *Some current challenges*

A number of critical matters need to be addressed, as we seek to go forward in mission in ways that are both faithful and renewed.

How can Anglican liturgy best provide worship that leads us, both as a community and as individuals, to the experience of the transcendent and triune God, the Father, the Son and the Holy Spirit? How can Anglicans best come to see worship as that which leads to holiness, and to an encounter with the holy God who calls us to be transformed in Christ?

How can we best facilitate the effective hearing of the Word, and ensure that we 'read, mark, learn and inwardly digest' it? How can congregations be better nurtured in the Word? How can worship best contribute to the continuing work of formation in the Christian life, to the fostering of holiness, and to a deep experience of God that will cause us to go out in mission?

Where is the Holy Spirit, and the spirit of celebration, encounter and response, in our worship? And how do we address the issues regarding our right discernment in the Spirit?

4.3. The future of Anglican worship

4.3.1. Building on the Prayer Book tradition

We will, as Anglicans, continue to cherish the Book of Common Prayer, mindful of its warning, in the section entitled 'Concerning the Service of the Church', that 'There was never any thing by the wit of man so well devised, or so sure established, which in continuance of time hath not been corrupted'. The work of Cranmer, in crafting the Prayer Book, provided a bridge to the ancient worship of the Church, which had adapted but not changed the heritage of Christian teaching informed by Holy Scripture. The Anglican *future* in worship lies in maintaining this theology and this approach, rather than pursuing a particular style, and also in the comprehensive task of holding on to all that is Scriptural and in the best of our tradition, as we believe and obey the Lord.

4.3.2. Continuity and adaptation

The matter of style should not be settled simply according to present-day patterns, just as, in the past, it has not been settled according to Biblical tradition alone. Instead, style in worship should reflect an encounter with the culture of a given time and place. The styles of Anglican worship will reflect who we are, peoples of one faith, and living in a multicultural, worldwide Communion. Yet there will be a family resemblance that will mark us out as Anglican. Cranmer had this in mind when he formulated Article 34, stating that 'It is not necessary that Traditions and Ceremonies be in all places one, and utterly like'. Nonetheless, we must not offend 'against the common order of the Church'. Forms of worship, therefore, are not to be imposed upon a people, which means that there is something refreshing and enriching about the diversity within our tradition.

In the future, Anglican worship should flourish if Anglicans continue to use their worship as an instrument of mission. In many situations, the regular repetition of the Anglican liturgy has been the principal means of teaching the faith in illiterate communities. This reminds us that worship is not dependent upon an elaborate intellectual grasp of the faith, and that the oral heritage of familiar and memorized prayers and texts, that we carry with us throughout our lives, is of the greatest value. So that it continues to be an instrument of mission, we must ensure that Anglican worship is always accessible to everyone, especially to children – 'From the lips of children and infants you have ordained praise' (Psalm 8:2) – and this would include the Eucharist itself.

Christians from all the Anglican Provinces and Dioceses can use their worship to bless other Christians, and the Anglican Communion, as they share what they have experienced of Christ, and also the way they have engaged in ministry in their local contexts. Music, of course, will help us in this.

4.3.3.   *The gift of music – enculturation and development*

God's great gift to us of music poses a challenge: how should we best employ it, knowing as we do that it is subject to cultural forces? Athanasius warned of the dangers of using artistic forms that are not capable of conveying divine truth. Music can be a vehicle of self-expression in many situations, but how can we use music in worship in such a way that it moves us, but does not leave us merely focused upon ourselves and our present enjoyment? Christian liturgy is inherently musical, and music may be used both to evoke and to express the feelings of worshippers. The Anglican liturgical tradition, in particular, helps us to remember the role of music as a vehicle for conveying God's majesty and compassion, as well as the great acts and truths of the faith. Yet it is clear that mere observance of a set formula will not create a living and authentic celebration of worship.

Music is always placed within a wider liturgical context, whether it be that of hearing the Word, a celebration of the Eucharist, Morning or Evening Prayer, or some other occasional service. The psalms and canticles with their antiphons, the hymns, responsories, litanies, acclamations, greetings and responses, and even the prayers, may all be greatly enhanced by music and by being sung.

It is important to preserve the overall integrity of the entire experience of worship, prayer and devotion. The various component elements in worship must therefore cohere with, and be subservient to, the wider whole, and be appropriate to the solemnity or festivity of the occasion. It is not appropriate to impose private meanings upon public worship, and this discipline applies as much to musical performance and performers as to anything else. The music employed must be fitting and conducive to worship, and not a distraction or impediment.

According to the local context, different languages will be appropriate, so that the people present will understand and connect with all that takes place in worship. Anything less would be contrary to the clear statement in Article 24: 'It is a thing plainly repugnant to the Word of God, and the custom of the Primitive Church, to have publick Prayer in the Church, or to minister the Sacraments in a tongue not understanded of the people.' The same thing might be said about different *styles* in worship, though here the issue would be enrichment, rather than understanding. Pastoral sensitivity will guide as to the needs of the people in a particular context. Classical hymnody, and Anglican psalm chant and responsorial singing, should continue to have their place as part of the great Anglican musical and choral tradition of excellence that has come down to us. We should also embrace contemporary music for our services, and local cultural traditions too, while seeking to maintain at all points the goal of excellence, remembering always that our music is an offering to God.

4.3.4. *Future challenges*

How can we best ensure the renewal of Anglican traditions of musical excellence? And how can we best engage with earlier, indigenous Christian traditions in music and liturgy, especially in places where ancient traditions continue in Anglican worship today? This is the case with the Coptic liturgy of St Basil, to name but one example. It should be remembered that Cranmer was influenced to some extent by the Eastern Orthodox liturgy, and later on the Liturgy of St John Chrysostom was to influence Lancelot Andrewes. Today, what can we learn from our differing church experiences of musical and liturgical practice? In recent times, for example, the worship of the Churches in North and South India has reflected elements from the earlier Rites of Bombay and Ceylon (Sri Lanka). What examples of excellence, from our many and various local contexts, could we share with each other?

How can we ensure that Anglican worship connects with the needs of the modern world? The diversity of patterns of worship, coming from around the Communion, includes occasional services – liturgies, benedictions and celebrations for the different stages of life's journey, from the cradle to the grave, and in accord with local needs. Liturgies must always speak to pastoral need, but the Book of Common Prayer of 1662 does not have everything that every context requires! Using modern technology, Anglicans can make available additional resources – obtained through appropriate mutual consultation, and with permission – so that sister churches and other Christian communities may better minister to a hurting world. Many other churches look to Anglicans for such resources, but Anglicanism itself has been blessed by the many and varied resources of others. The bands and processions of the Salvation Army, for instance, offer a vivid example of music being used in outreach.

We need many and varied resources to use in mission, as tools of ministry. In future, provision may be required to meet special liturgical needs. In an African context, these needs might include specific provision for rites of passage, and occasional services for special events, such as family and community occasions, agricultural seasons, and even industrial 'fixtures'. Of particular importance is the need to provide services with and for children; it is vital that children be truly and fully incorporated into the worshipping life of the Church.

4.4. *The unchanging goal of bringing all to Christ*

It is fitting to close this section with the words of Archbishop Cranmer himself, for they most eloquently disclose the force and urgency that lie behind our Anglican heritage, in liturgy and worship, as it seeks to bring all to Christ:

> When we hear Christ speak unto us with his own mouth, and shew himself to be seen with our eyes, in such sort as is convenient for him of us in this mortal life to be heard and seen; what comfort can we have more? The minister of the Church speaketh unto us God's own words, which we must take as spoken from God's own mouth, because that from his mouth it came, and his word it is, and not the minister's.

> Likewise, when he ministereth to our sights Christ's holy sacraments, we must think Christ crucified and presented before our eyes, because the sacraments so represent him, and be his sacraments, and not the priest's; as in baptism we must think, that as the priest putteth his hand to the child outwardly, and washeth him with water, so we must think that God putteth his hand inwardly and washeth the infant with his holy Spirit; and moreover, that Christ himself cometh down upon the child, and appareleth him with his own self: and at the Lord's holy table the priest distributeth wine and bread to feed the body, so we must think that inwardly by faith we see Christ feeding both body and soul to eternal life. What comfort can be devised any more in this world for a Christian man?[55]

---

[55] *An Answer by the Reverend Father in God, Thomas, Archbishop of Canterbury, Primate of all England, and Metropolitan, unto a Crafty and Sophistical Cavillation, devised by Stephen Gardiner, Doctor of Law, late Bishop of Winchester, against the true and godly doctrine of the most Holy Sacrament, of the Body and Blood of our Saviour Jesus Christ* (1551), Book Five (conclusion).

Our journey into the future

Over the past ten years the journey that we, as orthodox Anglicans, have taken together, has confirmed what we feared: some Churches in the Anglican Communion are radically redefining the received faith, and abandoning fundamental parts of it. We recognize that many in these Churches believe that the challenges they are making are Spirit-led, and necessary in order to respond to the challenges that the Church faces today.

Our own experience has been different. We have upheld the received biblical faith. We have found it to be relevant and powerful in addressing contemporary challenges. And we bear testimony to the gospel's transforming power, in our own lives and in our churches.

We have not claimed to possess the complete truth, but nor have we considered truth to be so provisional and partial, that one cannot possibly arrive at a clear judgment on theological error or unbiblical behaviour.

We recognize that the Holy Spirit of God leads God's people to truth, as they act and reflect together. We also recognize, however, that this is not just a continual process of listening and sharing, in which people are suspicious of judgments, and where there are no clear guidelines on discernment or on how to arrive at firm positions.

To deny the possibility of any access to the truth of God, suggests that God has been inadequate in making himself known to his own creation and to his creatures. It also means that final decisions, about what will count as truth in any given situation, remain with the powerful.

As those called to lead the Church, we have the

responsibility not just to testify to truth, but also to uphold it and commend it. But some in the Church, in their understandable desire not to exclude anyone's voice, especially the voices of individuals and groups who are seen as vulnerable and oppressed, are now making the inclusion of all voices, opinions and testimonies into the primary means whereby we experience and commend God's truth.

We note with deep sadness that such a view has led to a Church which includes much, but which does not recognize how it may have access to the truth of God. Therefore, having no good news about transformation of life, it has nothing to offer to the broken and disordered communities of our fallen creation.

Over the last ten years we have journeyed together in the search for a definition of faithful, orthodox Anglican identity. GAFCON is no new or reactive phenomenon. It is the culmination of years of witness, discussion, listening, engagement and prayer. The setting up of GAFCON came to be seen as a necessity, in order that we might meet together, affirm our identity as orthodox Anglicans, and identify the challenges to that identity, both from within the Anglican Communion and from without. We meet together as a people under Biblical authority, and as a people called to mission. We meet to maintain and to strengthen the unity of the Body of Christ.

We see a parallel between contemporary events and events in England in the sixteenth century. Then, the Catholic Church in England was faced with the choice of aligning itself with either Rome or Geneva. But, when forced to decide its identity, it sought to distinguish itself from both the practices of the Papacy and the excesses it associated with the more radical reformers. Now, after five centuries, a new fork in the road is appearing. Though this fork in the road may present itself publicly as a choice in relation to aberrant sexuality, the core issues are about whether or not there is one Word, accessible to all, and whether or not there is one Christ, accessible to all.

As we, in our time, face this dividing of the ways, we will need to depend absolutely upon God's guidance, discernment and judgment.

Jesus promised his disciples that the Holy Spirit would guide them into all truth (John 16:13). It is the Holy Spirit who provides the road map to truth, who leads God's people to the destination of truth. So we seek his guidance, in prayer together and through the Word, so as to identify the direction in which he is pointing us.

Discernment is to do with seeing reality as God intends us to see it, and clarifying how God calls us to respond to it. King Solomon sought the gift of discernment, as being the most necessary gift to lead God's people (1 Kings 3:9). He asks for a disposition of heart and mind that will enable him to discern God's purpose and act for the welfare of God's people.

When St Paul addresses the divisions in the church in Corinth (1 Corinthians chapters 1-3), he identifies the heart of the problem: God's wisdom and his purpose cannot be understood by human wisdom; they can only be 'spiritually discerned', by spiritual persons taught by the Spirit (1 Cor. 2:14-15). We come together to receive the Spirit's wisdom, a disposition of heart and mind that makes spiritual discernment possible.

We recognize in humility that we are called to share our testimonies of how God's truth judges and transforms us. We also recognize that we must uphold God's truth and act on it. Paul asks the Corinthians 'not to judge before the appointed time' (1 Cor. 4:5), but to wait till the Lord returns. However, this is not a call for inaction and endless process.

In the very next chapter, Paul does not hesitate to tell the Corinthian Church that he has already passed judgment on one of their members (1 Cor. 5:3). In prayer we seek God's judgment on his Church, and seek to act on that judgment. What might this look like in practice?

Firstly, action must be taken by leaders. The bishops of the Church are called to uphold her faith. In their relationship to the Spirit and the Holy Scriptures, they are a sign of the unity that God gives to the Church. So GAFCON is a meeting of bishops of the Church, with clergy and laity too, who seek God's way forward in our day, on the firm basis of the truth he has revealed.

Secondly, action has to be taken in public. The heroes of the faith, mentioned in the letter to the Hebrews, are celebrated for their public actions, not their feelings. Even when filled with fear, they overcame their intellectual and spiritual doubt, they discerned God's presence and will, and they acted on their faith. So GAFCON is, of necessity, a public gathering, because the issue at stake is the possibility of knowing the truth, and of obeying the truth in the public domain.

The possibility that there may be a truth that can be known is good news for people who want to see change. Those who deny that access to the truth is possible define everything in terms of power. Their own power, of course, is challenged by the very appeal to the higher court of truth.

The fundamental question is whether the Church *is* the message, or *has* the message. Some people want to say that the Church can share experience, and worship, and work, but that it cannot share faith because expressions of faith are so personal and diverse. So, they would say, the message of the Church is that its own diversity, and its ability to live with plurality and contradiction in its own membership on matters of faith, is precisely its witness in a plural society.

But the tensions and contradictions inherent in this position have become impossible to maintain. GAFCON is saying that there are Anglicans who are unwilling for the clarity of the Bible's message to be clouded by confusion, by those who directly contradict its teaching.

Our journey is witness that the truth of God is accessible. We are convinced that God has made himself known, sufficiently for us to be able to respond to him, and make truly moral choices between obedience and disobedience. This is critically important for evangelism among the poor.

Our journey has been to challenge those who would exercise institutional power to suppress the truth. We make this challenge in the name of God's love, and in order to honour the dignity and identity of the ordinary person, who does have access to God through the Scriptures.

Our journey is to seek our identity in relation primarily to that truth.

GAFCON identifies an area of public life today which is challenged to its heart by the gospel of the Lord Jesus. GAFCON is a statement that the truth of God can be known; that it is the gateway to fulfilling and fruitful life for men and women, in marriage or celibacy, and that obedience and witness to that truth cannot be confined to the space or the form that is offered by the powerful.

GAFCON is seeking to give public and institutional expression to the truth of the gospel in the public ordering of the Church. Far from accepting unlimited diversity and disobedience to the truth, this will mean respecting the order that God has given for authority in his Church and wholesomeness in society.

Bishops have responded to God's call to action by holding a public gathering at GAFCON. As they gather, they will look again to God's call for future action in faithful leadership of their Anglican Churches.

Glossary

AABC African Anglican Bishops Conference held in October 2004 in Lagos, Nigeria. www.aabc-ng.org

ACC The Anglican Consultative Council (ACC), established in 1968, facilitates the co-operative work of the Churches of the Anglican Communion, exchanges information between the Provinces and Churches, and helps to co-ordinate common action. It advises on the organization and structures of the Communion, and seeks to develop common policies with respect to the world mission of the Church, including ecumenical matters. The ACC membership includes from one to three persons from each province.
www. anglicancommunion.org

ACoC Anglican Church of Canada (www.anglican.ca).

Advocacy Groups A number of advocacy groups promote same-sex causes in the Anglican Communion: in the USA *Integrity,* in the UK and Nigeria *Changing Attitude* and *Lesbian and Gay Christian Movement.* Organizations and networks advocating faithfulness to Biblical teaching in this field are *Exodus* (www.exodus.to), *Living Waters* (www.living-waters-uk.org), *Redeemed Lives* (www.redeemedlives.org), *NARTH* (www.narth.com), www.pathinfo.org and www.peoplecanchange.com

Alternative Episcopal Oversight Arrangements whereby the oversight of a congregation is entrusted to a bishop who upholds the teaching of the Bible, as traditionally understood by the Churches of the Anglican Communion, this being a substitute for the geographical jurisdiction of the diocesan bishop, whose teaching or practice is contrary to the same.

AMiA Anglican Mission in the Americas, whose bishops sit in the House of Bishops of the Church of Uganda. www.theamia.org

CANA The Convocation of Anglicans in North America, an initiative of the Church of Nigeria which is under the oversight of bishops of the Church of Nigeria, and whose bishops sit in the House of Bishops of the Church of Nigeria. www.canaconvocation.org

CAPA The Council of the Anglican Provinces of Africa. CAPA has provided a forum for African Anglicans to meet and discuss common concerns.

Dar-es-Salaam Communiqué The official statement of the Primates' Meeting in February 2007. In particular it called for the cessation of lawsuits. See http://www.anglicancommunion.org/communion/primates/history/2007/index.cfm

ECUSA The Episcopal Church in the United States of America, now known as The Episcopal Church (TEC). www.ecusa.org

General Convention The Triennial Meeting of the Governing Body of The Episcopal Church (ECUSA/TEC).

Lambeth Conference The conference of all Anglican bishops held every ten years at the sole invitation of the Archbishop of Canterbury. Originally held at Lambeth Palace but now at the University of Kent at Canterbury. www.lambethconference.org

Lambeth Quadrilateral The following resolution was adopted by the Lambeth Conference of 1888:

The following Articles supply a basis on which approach may be by God's blessing made towards Home Reunion:

(a) The Holy Scriptures of the Old and New Testaments, as "containing all things necessary to salvation", and as being the rule and ultimate standard of faith.

(b) The Apostles' Creed, as the Baptismal Symbol; and the Nicene Creed, as the sufficient statement of the Christian faith.

(c) The two Sacraments ordained by Christ Himself – Baptism and the Supper of the Lord – ministered with unfailing use of Christ's words of Institution, and of the elements ordained by Him.

(d) The Historic Episcopate, locally adapted in the methods of its administration to the varying needs of the nations and peoples called of God into the Unity of His Church.

Orthodox Anglican Networks and Ecclesial Bodies These organizations advocate the transforming power of the Biblical gospel. In the USA they include the American Anglican Council (www.americananglican .org), the Anglican Communion Network (www.acn-us.org/), AMiA and CANA; in Canada, the Anglican Network in Canada (www.anglicannetwork.ca); in the UK, Anglican Mainstream (www.anglican-mainstream.net); globally, The Global South (www.globalsouthanglican.org) and Forward in Faith International (www.forwardinfaith.com); in Australia, The Anglican Church League (http://acl.asn.au/), and in South Africa, Anglican Mainstream Southern Africa (www.anglican-mainstream.org.za).

Primates Each of the 38 provinces of the Anglican Communion has one Primate who is an Archbishop or Presiding Bishop.

Primates' Meeting The meeting of the Primates established

in 1978, and one of the four instruments of unity. Given enhanced responsibility by the 1998 Lambeth Conference, its status has recently been called into question.
www.anglicancommunion.org/communion/primates/

TEC The new name for ECUSA (see above), adopted in 2006, in light of the fact that it had jurisdictions in 17 countries including Europe. www.ecusa.org

The Kigali Statement This was adopted by the meeting of the Global South Primates in Rwanda, September 2006. (http://www.globalsouthanglican.org/index.php/comments/kigali_communique/) It stated, 'We are convinced that the time has now come to take initial steps towards the formation of what will be recognized as a separate ecclesiastical structure of the Anglican Communion in the USA.'

The Road to Lambeth (2006) This document was prepared at Mukono, Uganda and commended for study by the Council of the Anglican Provinces of Africa. (http://www.globalsouthanglican.org/index.php/comments/the_road_to_lambeth_presented_at_capa/) It stated, 'We will definitely not attend any Lambeth Conference to which the violators of the Lambeth Resolution are also invited as participants or observers.'

The Windsor Report (2004) This was prepared by the Lambeth Commission, whose mandate spoke of the problems being experienced, as a consequence of the consecration of a practising homosexual person to the office of bishop in ECUSA, and of the need to seek a way forward which would encourage communion within the Anglican Communion. It sought to address the question of how the Anglican Communion should address relationships between its

93

component parts in a true spirit of communion. www.anglicancommunion.org/windsor2004/

To Mend the Net (2002) This was 'A Proposal for the Exercise of Enhanced Responsibility by the Primates' Meeting', put forward by two Primates, Archbishop Drexel W. Gomez (West Indies) and Presiding Bishop Maurice W. Sinclair (Southern Cone).

Websites Websites run by the American Anglican Council, the Anglican Church League, the Anglican Communion Network, CANA, AMiA, Anglican Mainstream and the Global South (see Orthodox Anglican Networks for web-addresses), the Church of Nigeria (www.anglican-nig.org), the Diocese of Sydney (http://www.sydneyanglicans.net) and Anglican Mainstream New Zealand (www.anglican-mainstream.org.nz/amnz), and the blogs of Babyblue, (www.babybluecafe.blogspot.com), Titusonenine (www.kendallharmon.net/t19), An Exercise in the Fundamentals of Orthodoxy (www.peter-ould.net), Stand Firm (www.standfirminfaith.com), and Virtueonline (www.virtueonline.org), enable concerned orthodox Anglicans to keep informed and prayerful.

Printed in the United States
206597BV00004B/289-525/P